Certainty for Life

AN INVITATION TO THOSE IN EASTERN ORTHODOXY

John Diacos

ARK
house

Ark House Press
arkhousepress.com

© 2025 John Diacos

Cataloguing in Publication Data:
Title: Certainty for Life
ISBN: 978-1-7643820-0-7 (pbk)
Subjects: REL030000 RELIGION / Christian Ministry / Evangelism; REL067100 RELIGION / Christian Theology / Soteriology; REL067030   RELIGION / Christian Theology / Apologetics.

Design by initiateagency.com

*For the glory of God
and the salvation of
Orthodox people everywhere*

TABLE OF CONTENTS

CHAPTER ONE

God's Search for me

Like every other Orthodox person I've met, I grew up without any certainty that I could be at peace with God. I knew all *about* God – our family's year revolved around Easter, and Saints' days, and Christmas, and regular attendance at Church. Being Orthodox was central to our cultural identity, which for me was Greek. Yet the picture of God presented to me was always one who disapproved of things I did. I did not know how to please or relate to this God at all. He was always distant, unapproachable, unknowable.

So, I searched in many directions for answers. I devoted myself to Church and ritual. I listened attentively to the liturgy, I kissed the icons, lit candles, and took communion. I always felt clean leaving Church, as if I had done my duty and that God was happy with me. But that feeling never lasted.

I devoted myself to doing good and developed a sensitive conscience that detected my inevitable failures. I would then pray with face to the ground, arms outstretched, sometimes with tears, begging for forgiveness until I believed I received it when I felt at peace. But I was never certain I was good enough, or that the forgiveness was complete.

So eager was I to know and be guided by God that I listened and looked at the world around me. I can remember being convinced that, any time I heard a sustained high-pitched sound, it was God telling me that he was near and cared for me. On another occasion I walked home from school in the rain without an umbrella, allowing it to drench me, because it felt as if the rain was God's presence around me.

Yet none of this left me with any certainty of knowing God, of having the truth, of feeling forgiven or of being at peace.

Maybe you have trodden down the same paths as me – or maybe entirely different ones. This book is to help you in your search. Or if you are not searching – this book is about why having answers to these questions about God is of ultimate importance.

This book is about finding those answers. It is about how we can have complete certainty of being forgiven by God, having peace, living the abundant life, and of life forever. It is about certainty because, in the end, I discovered that it was not about me and my performance, or even my search for God.

Instead, the liberating truth is that God is searching for *us*. That is why he sent his son Jesus, to find and rescue a lost humanity in order to offer them friendship and reconciliation. This is exciting news because it means that God is not far away. And because this is all God's initiative, reliant on him, then we can have certainty that he will make us clean and acceptable to him. We can know God personally and be welcomed into his family.

Why Read this Book?

In this book I want to present God's invitation to us to come to know him. As you read the chapters it will become apparent to you that we will be relying on the Bible to discover the truth. This is not a book written by an expert for experts. Yes, I do have degrees in theology, and can read the Bible in its original languages, but there are no hidden messages in the Bible that only academics can understand. The many modern translations of the Bible, with which we are now blessed, faithfully present God's words to us. For that is what the Bible is – God inspiring human writers over many centuries to deliver one united message from him to us. God speaks plainly to everyone – to the young and old, women and men, communicating clearly to people of all languages and cultures. God can do this for he is our creator who knows how we think, and he wants us all to know him. If only we will read it – which is what this book is all about.

As you read, perhaps some of these ideas will sound new to you. However, reading the Bible reveals to us God's most ancient message to humanity throughout history. It is one that has not changed over time but was the same to ancient Israelites as it was to the first Christians, and as it continues to be to us today. It has recorded for us what the original Church believed long before the formation of any denominations. In the Bible we will discover the unvarnished truth from God.

If you have doubts about the Bible being true or reliably transmitted from the originals, can I suggest you set aside those questions for now and start reading. I think the best way for you to assess the truth of the Bible is to read it, and see if it makes sense of God and humanity and the world.

All of the Bible passages include a reference to the location of those verses. Each reference to the Bible uses the name of the book as you will find it in a Bible. The two numbers at the end of the citation are the chapter and the verse.

So, 1 John 1:10 is the first letter of John, chapter 1, verse 10. Most of the time you will find the text of these verses within these pages. However, I encourage you to look up these passages yourself in a printed, online (for instance biblegateway.com), or on an app version of the Bible, of which there are many.

I have used the Christian Standard Bible (CSB) because not only is the translation faithful to the original languages in which the Bible was written, it is also fairly easy to read.

A Guide to Reading This Book

- **Part 1** considers why we need certainty, and the great problem we have towards God. We examine different ways we try to find God, and how God can be known.
- In **Part 2** we see how the Easter events are the solution provided by God. We look at how God has acted in Jesus to give us that certainty of forgiveness and life forever, that we all deeply need.
- **Part 3** looks at how we must respond to God, to accept his offer of forgiveness.
- **Part 4** is where the rubber really hits the road as we look at how we can start the new abundant life that God offers us.

The book is designed to be read from start to finish but you can also skip ahead to the sections that address your particular questions.

PART 1

The Unwelcome Certainty

CHAPTER TWO

Our Need for Certainty

Certainty in Life

Have you ever spent any time watching The Weather Channel? It features never ending analysis, reporting, predictions, science, and stories about – you guessed it – the weather. On the surface it sounds dull, unappealing and dry (pun intended). Yet even in competition with channels featuring live sport, the latest movies or comedy, The Weather Channel has always been one of the highest rating TV channels in the world.

Why? Because knowing what weather to expect gives us some certainty about the future. And we all desire certainty in our lives.

Certainty about the weather allows us to plan what to wear tomorrow, whether to take our umbrella, or to avoid travelling where there will be flooding. It helps us consider when it will be a good day for that next picnic, or whether we should change that to a lunch indoors. And don't I love to hear a forecast of a sunny, windy day on which to get the washing hung out.

However, there are more important matters of certainty in life than knowing whether to pack wet weather gear, or break out the shorts. We want to be sure about fundamentals – like knowing where your next meal is coming from, and that you will have a place to live. We desire the reassurance that we have secured regular work to pay for it all. We want the economy and prices to be stable. We want a country free from the disruption of war, riots, terrorism, or natural disasters. We would like the confidence that the rules and laws of society are just and clear, and applied equally to all. When we can have confidence in what to expect from the world around us, then we can plan for the future. Certainty gives us a sense of security over what tomorrow will bring. Certainty dispels our anxieties and fears.

Certainty in Relationships

Much more important than having certainty in the world is having it in those closest to us. We need friends and family on whom we can rely. The closer the relationship the more critical is this trustworthiness.

Marriage is the closest relationship between two people. In marriage we seek another who will be our partner in life. Ideally it will unite two people who will take their share of responsibilities in this new relationship. They commit to supporting one another emotionally and financially, and often to raise a family together. They promise to stand by one another, not only in the good times but especially in bad.

The lives of those who are married are so intertwined that they need to be sure they can rely on one another. So that, if one falls, they can look to the other to support them, no matter what. We need to be sure they will be on our side when everyone else has deserted us. To have someone like that who is always there for us makes us feel valued and loved. Each partner needs the other to be someone who keeps their promises, who is dependable. That gives us stability and security for we can have confidence in that relationship and in our lives together.

The more important the relationship, the more we rely on that person. The more important the relationship, the more devastating it is to us if they let us down. We need to have confidence in them, to have certainty in our most important relationships.

Certainty About God

How much more important is obtaining certainty when it comes to our relationship to God.

Yet, for many of us, God seems distant and unknowable. He is hidden from our sight and, indeed, from creation. When we go to Church, God can still seem far away, hidden behind ceremonies and unintelligible words. Some of us are told that only those with deep study and experience can know God, and we must trust them to instruct us. If all of this is true, how then can ordinary people like you and me come to know the God who is there?

Instead of certainty, all we have is questions. We would like to know God's character. Does he love us, does he look after us? Will he defend us against evil and injustice? Does God have any interest in us as individuals, and in our lives? Does God welcome relationship with him, and on what grounds? Can we earn God's favour with our sincerity, our good works, our religiosity or our self-denial? Can God be pleased at all or is it a futile effort? Does he want to know *us*?

We suspect God is all powerful – after all he is the God who made and rules the universe. We suspect that one day we will all have to give an account of our lives to him. The result of God's judgement will determine our eternal destiny. So we need the certainty that we are acceptable to God, that we are at peace with him.

But unless we know the truth about God we are left only with doubt. It leaves us with two options.

We can just give up – God is unknowable so I will just get on with my life. I might attend Church and family religious themed celebrations, but God will not impact my day to day living. But that is like ignoring a ticking time bomb and feeling safe because we put our fingers in our ears. If God is the judge whom we all must face, then we need to know the truth. We must be prepared.

So, the second option is activity. We might strive to do whatever we can to merit God's approval. But, once again, we lack certainty about what God desires from us. It means we can never know whether we are pleasing God, or even if we are on the right track. Driven by fear we strive harder and harder, hoping that God will accept us, yet never knowing if he will – which drives us even more. Unsure if our best is good enough, it makes us resentful of God. It leaves us anxious over death as we do not know what to expect in the afterlife.

My guess is that if you are reading this book, you are not ignoring God completely. You do want to know about him, and you know how important it is to be acceptable to him. But perhaps you are not sure about what God thinks of you – and you do not know whether you even can be.

A Critical Question

So, I want to pose you a question. It will help you to work out where you currently think you stand with God. Commit to your answer by making a note of it below or by writing it elsewhere.

The question is this:

> **If you were to die tonight and come before God, would he let you into His heaven?**

What do you think?

- ☐ Yes
- ☐ No
- ☐ I'm not sure
- ☐ Other

If you answered anything other than "Yes" then you have come to the right place. This book is for you. This book is for people who lack certainty about God, and who would like to obtain it.

Through the following chapters we are going to be considering what we can know about God, and giving answers to the questions I posed above. Most important of all, we are going to be answering the most significant questions anyone can ask:

Can I be sure of God's forgiveness?

Can I be sure of eternal life?

This aim of this book is to provide you with clear and definite answers to these questions about God. We are going to examine the conclusions about the certainty the first Christians came to so that we, too, can be certain. We will do that by examining the earliest of records of the original Church in the Bible.

In the Bible we will discover certainty regarding the most important relationship we can have with God. Having that certainty about God will liberate us from anxiety over the most significant aspects of our future. We will be freed from futile efforts at earning God's favour. Certainty will give us meaning and purpose in life and guide us into life to the full. Should you embrace that certainty, your life will never be the same again.

A WORD ABOUT TRADITION AND AUTHORITY

The Benefit of Experts

We obtain great benefit from experts. Those who have a deep understanding of their particular field, and are able to communicate that knowledge to us. The meteorologist who can interpret wind speeds, barometric pressures, and temperatures not only to tell us what to wear tomorrow, but warn us of dangerous weather events to avoid. The lawyer who can advise us how to act within the law, and be treated justly. The surgeon who can diagnose a life-threatening problem, and cure it.

In the same way we can benefit greatly from Christian experts. Not only those who would teach us now, but the experts from the past. We can learn much from the traditional teachings of the *Church Fathers*, as valued Christian teachers from the early centuries are called, that have been handed down to us over time. We benefit from their lives of faith and thought, as not only their writings, but also their influence, continues to guide us through to today.

For instance, the doctrine of the Trinity was worked out in the early centuries, as Christian leaders wrestled with, and discussed together, what the Bible had taught about Father, Son and Spirit. While some teachers took the lead, the doctrine was formulated over many years of consultation, back and forth between leaders. Two thousand years of Christian thinking has described a wide variety of doctrines – the traditional ways in which Christianity has been understood.

The benefit is that we can learn from their wisdom, their centuries of weighed and tested thoughts. It means we have a starting point from which to begin so we don't have to think through everything from the beginning.

Some have described the profit we gain from the past in this way: that though we are small, we can see far because "we stand on the shoulders of giants" as we benefit from the wisdom of those who came before.

Testing Tradition

As you read this book you will notice that, along the way, I incorporate several quotes from Church Fathers. I include these for their insightful and forceful reinforcement of the points we will see in the Bible. It also demonstrates that these are not new ideas, but were taught from the earliest days of Christianity. However, I have been selective. The reality is that I could easily produce a series of passages from the same, or equally respected, Church Fathers that make the completely opposite points. There is no uniformity in historical Christian doctrine. Traditions can be useful, but *they cannot all be true*. I do not think we have any difficulty imagining this to be the case when we hear the variety of different beliefs being taught as Christian today.

Yet, it would be impossible to discard the past for we have already been, and continue to be, influenced by it. Nor would it be practical to resolve to never listen to another Christian teacher. Plus, we would lose the wisdom of others. So we need to determine to whom we should listen. How should we assess those who seek to teach us, both from the past and presently?

I think this statement is helpful:

> "An astonishing number of religious groups today claim to be the successors of the early Church. A 'yardstick for truth' is needed by which to compare what the Church originally believed and practiced with what these groups proclaim."

> *What Orthodox Christians Believe* Conciliar Press, California, 1988, p1.

This makes sense to me. In order to weigh up the various doctrines which are presented to us, we need a measuring stick, a gold-standard that will tell us what is true.

Let's examine how Jesus assessed the teaching he encountered.

The Danger of Tradition

> Then Jesus was approached by Pharisees and scribes from Jerusalem, who asked, "Why do your disciples break the tradition of the elders? For they don't wash their hands when they eat."
>
> Matthew 15:1-2

The Pharisees were a group who were so committed in their service of God that they formulated their own encyclopaedia of rules to help them obey God's laws. Here they insisted that Jesus' disciples observe one of their hand washing rules. Importantly this is not about hygiene, nor even about obedience or acceptability before God. It's about observing their traditions and appearing acceptable before the community.

Jesus did not answer their question straight away for, as usual he confronted them with the real issue.

> He answered them, "Why do you break God's commandment because of your tradition? For God said: **Honour your father and your mother;** and, **Whoever speaks evil of father or mother must be put to death.** But you say, 'Whoever tells his father or mother, "Whatever benefit you might have received from me is a gift committed to the temple," he does not have to honour his father.' In this

way, you have nullified the word of God because of your tradition."

Matthew 15:3-6

Jesus cites another of their traditions to demonstrate their error. In the time before pensions and social security, children had a responsibility to care for their parents in their old age. But the Pharisees introduced a loophole. Commit the money you would otherwise provide for your parents to the Temple, and you are free from your obligation. It had the advantage of making them look pious for giving to the Temple and would show them to be devoted to the worship of God. What made this abuse worse was that the money did not actually have to be given – it only had to be committed to the Temple at some future time, say in a will, maybe never to be enacted. So, it was nothing more than words – the words that deprived their parents of the support they deserved, in preference to those children being well thought of by their neighbours.

Even on the surface this was despicable selfishness. But, worse than that, was what it demonstrated was the real reason for their enthusiasm for tradition.

So, Jesus declared:

"Hypocrites! Isaiah prophesied correctly about you when he said: **This people honour me with their lips, but their heart is far from me. They worship me in vain, teaching as doctrines human commands."**

Matthew 15:7-9

This is a damning condemnation from Jesus. Their rules made them look like they were zealous for God, when it was actually the opposite. The word of God was clear – honour your father and mother, but their rule resulted in them side-stepping that responsibility. Their actual intention was to *avoid* obeying God. They constructed regulations to *minimise* their obligation to God.

Most importantly, if they were obedient to their own interpretations instead of to God, who were they actually serving? Not God. They were serving themselves, obeying their own rules rather than God's. Their interpretations overruled the clear word of God.

The disciples were shocked that Jesus could say such things about these admired religious teachers. But Jesus goes further.

> "Leave them alone! They are blind guides. And if the blind guide the blind, both will fall into a pit."
>
> Matthew 15:14

It is an evocative statement that has passed into the English language. When the blind come seeking guidance it will do them no good being led by another who is similarly blind. The Pharisees have blinded themselves to God by giving their own interpretations authority over his word. Have nothing to do with them, says Jesus. They cannot lead their followers to God but only into the same disastrous pit of judgement into which they are headed.

Jesus' Yardstick

Jesus makes clear here how he thinks of the Scriptures. He quotes the words of Exodus that says 'honour your father and mother' but Jesus states that they are actually God's words. Jesus does this every time he quotes the Bible. And, according to Jesus, as they are the words of God they come with the *authority* of God. They cannot be overruled by anyone's interpretations.

This is Jesus' yardstick against which all teachers, and their doctrine, are to be assessed: how closely they reflect the Biblical word of God. Jesus measured the Pharisees against this gold-standard, and following Jesus it is how we ought to continue measuring teachers today.

The Original Church and Apostolic Succession

However, you may ask, what did the original Church believe? What about the idea of an *Apostolic Succession* – that an unbroken line of teaching has been passed down from the beginning from the Apostles to the next generation to the next until it has reached us?

These are the instructions the apostle Paul provides to his student, Timothy:

> "What you have heard from me in the presence of many witnesses, commit to faithful men who will be able to teach others also."
>
> 2 Timothy 2:2

Paul is describing how this Apostolic succession should operate. As an apostle, Paul has taught the very word of God, both in speech and, in this instance, by letter. Timothy is to take these Apostolic words and teach others who can pass them on.

What is critical here is not the process. There is no guarantee that the very act of succession will mean the truth is preserved. What is critical is that the original message – "what you have heard" – is passed on. Timothy is not free to change the message, nor is anyone after him. That is why the men, to whom it is passed, must above all be faithful – so they can be trusted to preserve and repeat *the same message* as it was given to them.

However, human beings are fallible. God is perfect but, try as much as we might, all people make mistakes (I just made one now typing the word "mistake"!). We mishear, misunderstand, and are forgetful. People are also sinful. It means that, consciously or not, we may change the doctrine we received to better suit our liking. All this means we can never be sure that what we are taught is the original message.

Many people played the game 'Telephone' as children. It is where children stand in a row, and the first child whispers a message to the second child, who whispers it to the third, and so on until the end of the line. The message reported by the last child is then compared to the original message. Usually, the words have been misheard and incorrectly repeated, and the final message bears little comparison to the first. The transmission cannot be considered as successful merely because there was an unbroken line, and something was reported in the end. Success requires the final message to be the same as the first. The only way to determine that is by comparing the received message with the original.

In the same way the truth cannot be guaranteed by simply tracing a line between the early Church and today. It is not enough to claim continuity with the original Church. To assume authority based on a particular set of traditions would be to do the very thing for which Jesus condemned the Pharisees.

Thankfully we do not have to rely on playing Telephone. The Bible accurately records for us the teaching of the Apostles to the early Church. We can know the truth with certainty.

Final Authority Rests with the Word of God

The Bible is the gold-standard yardstick provided by God himself. As the word of God, it is the final authority in all matters of faith. So, to assess

Christian teaching, like the ideas in this book, we must measure them against the Biblical word of God. To know whether traditional doctrines have been faithfully transmitted from the early Church – we need to compare them to Scripture.

Here are wise words from one of those Church Fathers:

> "We have known the method of our salvation by no other means than those by whom the gospel came to us; which gospel they truly preached; but afterward, by the will of God, they delivered to us in the Scriptures, to be **for the future the foundation and pillar of our faith**,"
>
> Irenaeus (AD 130-202) *Against Heresies*
> Book 3 ch 1 para 1 (emphasis mine)

We can learn much from those who are wiser and more experienced. Traditional and historical beliefs, and present-day teachers, all have a place, and can give us great benefits. The best Christian traditions and doctrines will introduce us to ideas we might never have discovered on our own. But the views we will encounter about God, and truth, are as many as there are individuals in the world. That means that ancient quotes can be found to support any position. But something is not true because it is ancient – it may just be an old lie. Something is not true because many people said it – truth is not determined democratically, and many are the instances when the majority of people have been in error. Something is not even true when a reliable witness, like an early Church Father, has declared it. For some of them have made many mistakes; but all of them have made some mistakes. For even the greatest of Church Fathers were sinful men.

So where are we left in our pursuit of truth? Should you believe everything I write? No, for I too am sinful and imperfect. How about all the Church Fathers I have been quoting? The same goes for them. We must never forget that they, too, are human, and that their doctrines can never be permitted to overrule God's Biblical and apostolic word. God must always be the final authority in all matters of Christian doctrine. The only reliable statement of truth is the one where God reveals himself to us – in his word, the Bible.

God has not left us in darkness but has given us his word so we can know him. Not that all the Bible is equally easy, but God's truth about himself and us, and his plan to rescue us from sin and death, is clear for all to understand.

CHAPTER THREE

Ungrateful Children

What did Jesus think about sin?

During the time when Jesus became well known, he attracted great popularity and many listeners. However, the truth he taught about God also challenged the established religious teachers who questioned the purity of Jesus' views. The Apostle Luke's account of Jesus' life describes one occasion in this way:

> All the tax collectors and sinners were approaching to listen
> to him. And the Pharisees and scribes were complaining,
> "This man welcomes sinners and eats with them."
>
> Luke 15:1-2

Jesus did not restrict himself to the religious, the pure, and the upright members of society. Not only did he have something to say to those whose lifestyles were condemned by those around them, Jesus spent time with them. He would even eat with them.

The process of eating is, itself, merely the consumption of food for energy – and anyone can eat on their own. But eating with someone else is a significant social activity. Eating with another is a relationship building activity, that indicates we are aligned and united with them. It is what we do with friends and family, and how we build our relationships with them. For the same reason eating is what we avoid doing with enemies.

Anyone who has ever allocated wedding reception seating knows the headache of trying to keep apart all the relatives who no longer speak to one another. And every week scorn is poured upon celebrities or politicians when photos are published of them dining with infamous criminals in their houses, or celebrating their birthdays or wedding. To eat with someone declares your unity with and sympathy towards them.

So the shocking accusation being levelled at Jesus by the religious leaders – the Pharisees and scribes – is that, by eating with sinners, Jesus sympathises with them. Does Jesus therefore approve of their lifestyle? In other words they ask, does Jesus take sin seriously?

Jesus answers them with a story about an ungrateful son.

An Ungrateful Son

"A man had two sons. The younger of them said to his father, 'Father, give me the share of the estate I have coming to me.' So he distributed the assets to them.

Luke 15:11-12

It is a story of a young man who cannot wait to spend his inheritance. Not only does he not want to wait for the Will to be read, but he also cannot wait until his father has died. So he approaches his father and, in effect, asks: "do I really have to wait until you die to get my money?" In other words, he declares to his father's face, "I wish you were dead".

Remarkably, his father acquiesces to his request. There is no heated argument, the father does not kick him out of the house, or beat him, or tell him to get a job and earn his own money. Instead, he generously gives. Somehow the father liquidates his assets. Perhaps he mortgages his land, sells off his animals and his possessions to give this younger son his inheritance.

Then this happens:

> Not many days later, the younger son gathered together all he had and travelled to a distant country, where he squandered his estate in foolish living.
>
> Luke 15:13

The son's contempt for his father is underlined by what happens next. He is more than happy to take his father's money. But then he wants to get as far away as possible – to a *distant* country.

It really is all about the money for this son, as he proceeds to quickly spend it. The adjective translated 'foolish' here is the Greek word *asotos* (ἀσώτως) which means his living is *expensive and wasteful*. His father has given him money, which is good and needful to eat and live. He should be grateful and thankful for his father's generosity. But the son demonstrates he doesn't appreciate the value of what he has been given by the way he fritters it all away.

> After he had spent everything, a severe famine struck that country, and he had nothing. Then he went to work for one of the citizens of that country, who sent him into his fields to feed pigs. He longed to eat his fill from the pods that the pigs were eating, but no one would give him anything.
>
> Luke 15:14-16

With his money all gone, and there is a famine in the land, the son is left in need. So hungry is he that he not only takes a job tending the pigs, but would have eaten their food if he could. Of course, Jews consider pigs to be unclean animals. So, for the audience hearing this story, the son is suffering the ultimate humiliation of not only living amongst the pigs, but of wanting to eat their food. He has rejected his own people, and is now being abandoned by the people with whom he chose to live.

> When he came to his senses, he said, 'How many of my father's hired workers have more than enough food, and here I am dying of hunger! I'll get up, go to my father, and say to him, "Father, I have sinned against heaven and in your sight. I'm no longer worthy to be called your son. Make me like one of your hired workers."'
>
> Luke 15:17-19

The son finally realises the desperate position in which he finds himself – broke and without food, family, or friends. He arrives at the conclusion that reveals how he has been thinking all along. In the beginning all he wanted was his father's money. When he had money, his life was all about spending it. Now that it is gone, and he is hungry, his solution is to get more.

So, because he knows his father pays his workers well, he decides to return. For the son it's simply and only about economics – nothing else. There is no admission from the son that he has done wrong, no recognition that he broke his father's heart, no regret at abandoning his family, or at wasting away half of their estate. His rehearsed speech for his father is merely to facilitate his acquisition of a well-paid job. From the beginning until now he has only thought about himself, taking what he can get and thanking no-one.

What has the son done?

We leave this story here. We will return to consider Jesus' conclusion to it in Chapter Fifteen.

However, in this first part, what is Jesus suggesting has been the error of this son? It is that everything this son has was given to him by his father. He was generously provided with all that he needed, and without question. He did not have to earn it, like his father's workers. He was given it freely because he was a beloved son. But, despite all of this, he is not thankful, he does not recognise his father's love expressed in his generosity towards him, or the sacrifices that have been made to give him what he needs. He is never satisfied, and only wants more. Rather than give his father the love and respect he deserves, he wishes him dead.

This is a model of ingratitude. Of thanklessness towards others. Of deep-seated selfishness.

This is a story about us

But this is not the story of a dysfunctional family, or one wicked son. This is a story about fundamental human nature. For in the picture of the young man, Jesus is illustrating what the Bible calls sin. At its heart, sin describes our selfishness and ungratefulness towards God.

We too have a generous loving father in God. He made us all. The universe in which we live, the food we eat, our family and friends – everything that is good comes from him.

But we are like the son. We are never satisfied with what God provides for us. We fail to respond to God's goodness to us with the love and respect he merits. We want to pretend that we deserve all, and have earned all that we have. We wish God were not there, interfering in our lives and telling us what to do.

All of us are God's ungrateful children, and that is sin.

Sin is Ingratitude towards God

Hear what God has to say to us about sin in Paul's letter to the Romans:

> For God's wrath is revealed from heaven against all godlessness and unrighteousness of people who by their unrighteousness suppress the truth, since what can be known about God is evident among them, because God has shown it to them. For his invisible attributes, that is, his eternal power and divine nature, have been clearly seen since the creation of the world, being understood through what he has made. As a result, people are without excuse.
>
> Romans 1:18-20

The universe itself loudly declares the power and presence of the divine creator behind it all. It speaks of the one who created the entire universe of matter and energy from nothing, and designed it all with incredible precision and complexity. It announces the God who made the stars, and guided them on their course to where they are, who manages the thermonuclear reactions in the Sun to provide us with light and heat, who cloaked our planet with an atmosphere to protect it, and placed the Earth at the precise distance and angle from the Sun such that even the smallest percentage of deviation would have made life on Earth impossible.

This is the one who made the mountains, as well as the valleys along which the rivers flow. He sculpted the continents and the islands, and divided land from water. God made the broad diversity of plants and animal life, and he made human beings. He made the amazing wonder of our bodies, with a nervous system that contains every thought and controls every muscular function, both voluntary and involuntary, even down to the microscopic detail of our eyes and ears. God made the wonderful saddle joint of your thumb, that allows it to turn in 360 degrees and be opposable to all your other fingers to enable us to grasp and handle tools. He made the complexity of a circulatory system with its 10,000 km of conduits. Within them God made the multifunctional blood cells, and the soup in which they swim so that it is difficult to imagine how else complex multi-cellular organisms could exist without a system for transporting oxygen, and the multiple other nutrients, hormones and enzymes they require.

There are no subtle hints in the universe. There is nothing around us that does not bear God's fingerprints, and it is obvious to us all. As verse 19 above says, all people everywhere have the inherent knowledge that the creator God exists.

Here in Australia, I can see that most people accept God's existence by how confidently they blame him when something goes wrong – and also by how readily they pray to him in times of crisis. Indeed, most arguments for 'atheism' arise from disappointment with a God who does not run the world in the way we think he ought. In other words, rather than an argument for God's non-existence, it is more an expression of anger with the God whom we all know is there.[1]

---

[1] For example, the argument that, in a world of suffering, a good God cannot exist. The argument assumes we know at least as much about the world as an all-knowing deity, so can determine what is good and just for the world – but it also assumes that such a deity exists who controls the world. If the argument is correct, and there is no God, then against whom can we direct our complaint about suffering? Without God, good and evil and suffering become meaningless, and even illusory categories.

However, despite knowing God is our creator, *all of us* 'suppress the truth' (verse 18). The God to whom we owe everything is to us, to borrow Al Gore's phrase, is 'an *inconvenient* truth'. None of us can afford to admit that all we have comes from God. For, if we were to do that, we would also have to acknowledge that he is our owner and ruler and knows best how we ought to live.

But we do not want that. We want to be in control, independent of all others, and in charge of our lives so we can live as we wish. Like the son who wished his father was dead, we wish God was not there telling us what to do.

God's word in Romans then describes the result:

> ... though they knew God, they did not glorify him as God or show **gratitude**. Instead, their thinking became worthless, and their senseless hearts were darkened.
>
> Romans 1:21
> (emphasis mine)

There is that word – *gratitude*. Our fundamental failure towards God is being ungrateful. After all God has done in creating us, and richly providing us with all we need, we reject him as our owner and ruler. We take everything God gives us and treat him with utter contempt by ignoring him. Like the younger son acted towards his father, so we all act towards God – like ungrateful children.

How God responds

How should God respond to our ingratitude towards him?

I expect that all of us have close or personal experience of dysfunction, either within our families or those of our wider family and friends.

There are families where their members no longer communicate with one another. Where, instead of the strongest of relational bonds that should exist between parents and child, there is hostility and enmity. The fault usually lies with both parent and child, at least in part. On both sides there may have been harsh words, offences, and pride involved.

But what about the circumstance where there is a loving parent? One who deeply loves their child and does anything and everything for them. Who protects them, provides them with all they need, who only wants what is good for their child, no matter the cost. What do we make of the child who receives all of that, yet nevertheless hates their parent? One who resents their parents' support and rejects their love. One who wishes their parent would no longer interfere, that they would cease to exist.

In that case, we should have profound contempt for the deep betrayal of such an ungrateful child. We would be appalled at someone who failed to appreciate the benefits of having such a loving parent. We would recognise that it this child's actions which have broken their relationship to their parent. We would agree that their parent should be disappointed and angry.

This is the story that Jesus told of the younger son—a son who deserves his father's anger and has no right to expect to be welcomed back.

Of course, Jesus' story is an illustration of humanity's relationship with God. Our Father God has shown us love and generosity, by creating us and richly supplying us with all that is good. Yet, like the ungrateful son, we have taken from our Heavenly Father, and have not lived a life of serving and thanking him.

What do we deserve from God? God's word that we read above in Romans tells us that, "**God's wrath** is revealed from Heaven against all godlessness and unrighteousness of people who by their unrighteousness suppress the truth".

'Wrath' means anger, fury. **God is angry with us**. It is an appropriate response to our ingratitude towards him.

But we have done worse than being ungrateful to God.

Sin is Destructive

For, by refusing to allow God to interfere in our lives, we live as we please. We ignore God's good instructions for life. Instead all of us have run our lives our own way, without God. We live self-centredly by doing what we think is best for ourselves, and the people and things we love. And just like the younger son fleeing to a distant land and spending his fortune, we have made a mess of our world.

> And because they did not think it worthwhile to acknowledge God, God delivered them over to a corrupt mind so that they do what is not right. They are filled with all unrighteousness, evil, greed, and wickedness. They are full of envy, murder, quarrels, deceit, and malice. They are gossips, slanderers, God-haters, arrogant, proud, boastful, inventors of evil, disobedient to parents, senseless, untrustworthy, unloving, and unmerciful. Although they know God's just sentence – that those who practice such things deserve to die – they not only do them, but even applaud others who practice them.
>
> Romans 1:28-32

Paul is describing the world he sees in the Roman Empire in the middle of the 1st Century. But the world is no different today. The modern media lists the constant violence, wars, terrorism, and riots. Parents, who are supposed to care for their children, are abusing them emotionally, physically, or even just abandoning them. Children, like the younger son, who are supposed to respect and honour their parents are, instead, fighting against them and ignoring them. Husbands and wives are at war, and families battle over inheritances. Then there is racism, sexual exploitation, addictions, poverty, theft, murder, road rage, corruption – the list goes on. Within ourselves there is turmoil and discontent. Even the best of our efforts is corrupted by self-centred motivations. As long as we are alienated from our creator, God, nothing can go completely right.

We are like a foolish fish that thinks it knows better than to swim in water, so it chooses to jump out. For, by rejecting our maker's instructions in favour of our own life choices, we have only made things worse. The futility of such thinking is demonstrated by the resultant mess we have made of our lives and our world.

All of us are to blame

We have all acted in this way, living life for ourselves. If we are honest with ourselves, we will admit that we have said and done things that have harmed others. Sometimes it is on purpose; sometimes it is out of carelessness or is unintentional. We have broken promises and let people down. We have become angry, or spoken discouraging and hurtful words, or gossiped, or lied to protect ourselves. We have all mistreated others, been unfair, even exploited and taken from others what is not rightly ours. Then there are those things of which we are ashamed and embarrassed that we do not want to admit to anyone, even ourselves. Yet none of it is hidden from God.

It will do us no good to complain that others have done worse than us. For whether we have played a large part or small, the world is in a mess, and we are part of the problem. *We* are what is wrong with the world.

Our Relationship with God is broken

So, what do you think now? Now that we understand that we have turned our back on God, and messed up his good creation, will God welcome us into his Heaven?

We do not have to guess at the answer, for God gives it to us very clearly:

> For all have sinned and fall short of the glory of God
>
> Romans 3:23

> …when he takes vengeance with flaming fire on those who don't know God and on those who don't obey the gospel of our Lord Jesus. They will pay the penalty of eternal destruction from the Lord's presence…
>
> 2 Thess 1:8-9

Sin is our declaration of independence from God. By our own choice we have separated ourselves from God. The result is that we will get exactly what we have chosen. God will not admit us into his presence.

Breaking a relationship always means losing the benefits of that relationship. Leaving a job means losing the pay and benefits the employer provides. We would no longer expect wages or superannuation contributions, sick days or annual leave, access to the office or company property, or a login to their computers. The younger son in Jesus' story, having cut himself off from his father, eventually finds himself far from home, sitting in the filth with the pigs and with nothing to eat.

Similarly, rejecting God means forfeiting all of the good things God would give us.

Without God's blessings we will have none of the good things we now enjoy – no food, water, clothing, shelter warmth, or friends, family and love, or sleep, relaxation and holidays, or joy, laughter, or *life*. That the destruction will be 'eternal' describes not so much the length of time as much as the extent – that this destruction will be complete, without hope of recovery.

Separation from God and his goodness is what the Bible calls Hell. It is a fitting punishment for our ingratitude, at having turned our back on the God who supplies all that is good.

> Life there is so unbearable that it is impossible to comprehend clearly the misery caused by the deprivation of God's good things.
> John Chrysostom, Archbishop of Constantinople
> (d AD 407), *Homily 23 (7) on Matthew (c. 307-407)*

Sin is deadly serious

We can now see how this story of Jesus has addressed his attitude towards sin. In his story Jesus is saying what the rest of God's word to us says. Sin is a deadly serious problem for all of us. It separates us from God now, and will be separate us from his goodness eternally.

As a doctor I have often had to inform a patient of a serious diagnosis. It is dreadful for them to hear, and I take no joy in delivering the news. However, the truth must be told. In fact, their only hope for a cure is in receiving an accurate diagnosis. For only then can the appropriate intervention be identified and applied, and there be hope for recovery.

So too here. The certain condemnation of God upon us is the worst diagnosis any of us receives. But it is the truth. And, with this truth, comes hope. For only by knowing the problem will we be driven to seek out the solution.

What can be done?

So, what can be done? Now that we have an accurate diagnosis of our problem with God, what is the solution?

Is it a matter of trying harder? Or should we instead shut ourselves off from the world so we can fast and pray?

Chapters Four and Five consider these options.

CHAPTER FOUR

What if I Try Harder?

Qualifying for the Olympics

As I write this, the Olympics is about commence. It will feature the best athletes in the world competing for gold for their respective sports. You must be the best in your country to qualify, to participate in the Olympics, and even better to win.

I was a fair sprinter in my youth. I once ran 100 metres in around 12 seconds (it was so long ago I think they timed it with a sundial). Of course, that would only get me entry to an Olympics as a spectator.

In Australia we get excited about any 100-metre sprinter who can break 10 seconds. They travel to the Olympics with the hopes of a nation behind them – but that time might not even get them into the final.

Usain Bolt was the greatest 100-metre runner to date. He holds the current world record of 9.58 seconds and won three gold medals.

Could I ever run that fast? Not a chance. No matter how hard I trained or tried, irrespective of the quality of my coach, the only way I'm travelling that rapidly is in a car. No medals for me.

How about our sub-10 second hero? They have a much better chance. Training, diet, weights, strategy. Of course, all their competitors will be training just as hard. Yet even for them there is a limit to how much they can improve, no matter how hard they train or try. Maybe they cannot get any faster. Perhaps no medals for them as well.

How good is good enough for God?

Is that how it works for God? Try hard, do your best, and maybe win the prize? How good is good enough for God? What is his cutoff for qualification?

Jesus had a direct answer to those who wanted to be good enough for God in his Sermon on the Mount.

> I tell you, unless your righteousness surpasses that of the scribes and Pharisees, you will never get into the kingdom of Heaven.
>
> Matthew 5:20

As we saw before, the Pharisees were seriously religious people. They worked hard to not only remember, but to obey the 613 rules they had identified in the Old Testament. They were so serious that rule 613 was to wear a shawl with tassels that included 612 knots to remind them of those commandments.

They were so serious that they invented rules to help them keep the *other* rules. God required a tenth of everything that a person produced – so the Pharisees insisted that every patch of parsley and mint also have a tenth of them devoted to God. Touching a dead body made you unclean so, to make extra sure, the Pharisees taught to not even let your shadow touch a dead body.

One of the ten commandments was to keep the Sabbath day (Saturday) as a day of rest. So the Pharisees literally made hundreds of rules so that no one would do any unintentional work on the Sabbath. One rule said you could not walk through a field on the Sabbath because your sandal might clip a grain of wheat and, if it did, you would be harvesting grain! Nor could you spit on the ground because your spit would create mud, and this was making mortar used in building. You could not swat a fly, for then you would be guilty of hunting. The Pharisees thought deeply, and carried out their obligations to God so their lives might please him.

Yet Jesus shockingly says – you must be more religious than the Pharisees; work harder than them if you want to have any chance of getting into Heaven.

Jesus reminds them of the commandment 'do not murder' in order to suggest that being angry with another person is just as bad, and will face the same judgement[2]. Jesus says not only are we commanded 'do not commit adultery' but, just thinking lustfully about another, also breaks that command[3]. Jesus says that if anyone slaps your cheek, give him the other to hit as well, and to love your enemies and pray for them[4]. It is not just behaviour that has to fall into line with God's commands, but our private thoughts as well. The Pharisees cannot meet these standards – nor can any of us.

In fact, the apostle Paul was himself trained as a Pharisee. He personally lived out this disciplined life, and zealously tried to obey all of God's laws, in addition to the Pharisaic rules, in an attempt to please God. Yet as he reflected on the result of those strenuous efforts, his lifetime devoted to trying his hardest to be good enough for God, Paul concluded that the

---

[2] Matthew 5:21
[3] Matthew 5:27-28
[4] Matthew 5:39

very best of his good works were nothing more than dung (or excrement)[5]. His very best efforts, at trying to be good enough for God, deserved to be flushed down the toilet. Not even the super righteous Pharisees, who devoted their whole lives to obeying the law of God, could do enough to please him.

It would be like saying that Usain Bolt didn't deserve a gold medal – come back when your 100-metre time breaks 5 seconds. It's simply an impossible task to work harder than the Pharisees at keeping God's law.

So, what does Jesus conclude about how good you have to be to earn acceptability before God?

> Be perfect, therefore, as your heavenly Father is perfect.
> Matthew 5:48

God is our creator who gives us everything we have. The air we breathe, the shelter under which we live, the food we eat, the water we drink, the clothes we wear, our families and friends, and the Sun and the rain – and even our very lives. He deserves for us to serve him as our God, to obey him completely.

So if you want your goodness, your obedience before God, to be what makes you acceptable to God, then Jesus makes it clear – you will have to keep God's law perfectly. Every day we owe God our perfect service.

But that is impossible. Every day we fail. Every day we are in debt to God for the service we have not given him. As we can never offer a day of perfection, our debt to God continues to accrue. We have an un-repayable debt to God, and we owe more daily. We have no hope of striving hard enough to repay God, to please him through our obedience.

---

[5] Philippians 3:8

I was raised with a strong work ethic. I always want to undertake my responsibilities by doing them myself, rather than asking or paying someone else to do it. I take great joy in being able to complete a project, and then to sit back and appreciate the fruits of my labour. Work is a good gift of God, and there is great satisfaction in carrying out tasks yourself. However, sometimes I am not qualified to do a job, like doing electrical or plumbing work. Other tasks, like lifting and moving a house by my own strength, are beyond my abilities to complete.

Attempting to please God is like trying to lift that house. It does not matter how much pride I take in accomplishing things myself, or in not relying on anyone else. It is impossible. No matter how hard I work, I can never do enough to please God.

What About Religion?

What then about the role of religion? Religion teaches us God's laws and encourages us to obedience. Doesn't religious devotion draw us closer to God? Can't religious rules save us?

Writing to the Roman Christians, the apostle Paul declares that God's law is good:

> I would not have known sin if it were not for the law. For
> example, I would not have known what it is to covet if the
> law had not said, Do not covet.
>
> Romans 7:7

The law describes God's good requirements for us. It draws a boundary around what is acceptable behaviour, what is beneficial for us and the world. Everything outside that boundary is harmful to us. That's why God warns us against it.

But we think we know better than God. We all reject God's rule over us and do what we want to do instead. We want to act outside the boundaries set for us by God's laws – that's what sin is. Sin means we cannot accept God's law as being for our own good. In fact, so perverse are we in our thinking, we reason that by his rules God is trying to stop us from doing good things. So, if God tells us how to live, instead we want to do the opposite.

Here is how the apostle Paul describes it:

> And sin, seizing an opportunity through the commandment, produced in me coveting of every kind. For apart from the law sin is dead. Once I was alive apart from the law, but when the commandment came, sin sprang to life again and I died. The commandment that was meant for life resulted in death for me.
>
> Romans 7:8-10

God tells us to not covet – not to desire those things that belong to someone else. To indulge thoughts of how much better other people have it, produces in us anger and bitterness, and destroys our relationships with others. God's command is for our good.

However, our sinfulness has corrupted our thinking. When God says "no" we do not thank him for warning us away from danger. Instead, because we doubt God's goodness, we assume he must want to stop us from having good things. I never thought before about taking what is not mine, but being told not to makes me wonder what I am missing out on! So rather than stopping me, my perverse sinfulness twists God's good laws and incites me to break them.

This is why those things which are forbidden are immediately attractive to us. Advertising copywriters understand this principle. "Drink Maxwell

Coffee – It Tastes So Good It's Sinful." The claim about the quality of the coffee is debatable, but the implication in suggesting its great taste is comparable to sin is clear – we believe sin is good. Then consider 'taste the forbidden fruit' (which is for what must be *really* delicious chewing gum) or the slogan for the fragrance 'Temptation' which predictably invites us to "Indulge in the irresistible allure of Temptation". Or how about the countless places around the world dubbed 'Sin City'. They are so called because they cater to a wide variety of vices. However, the title Sin City serves not to repel, but to attract visitors. These associations with 'sin' and 'forbidden' all capitalise on our suspicion that anything prohibited must be good. So, instead of stopping us, the law that says 'don't' has the opposite effect of making disobedience more desirable.

I have a very clear memory at age four of being strongly told by my mother not to touch the hot steam iron. I remember nevertheless reaching up with my little hand, curious to experience the good thing that was forbidden to me. I very quickly discovered that my mother's rule was not denying me good but was for my protection. (Don't be concerned – there was no lasting damage.)

I never touched a hot iron again. But, learning that rules can be for my good, did not stop me challenging my mother again. Nor did it stop me from defying the laws of God, even though his commands are *always* for our best.

The result is that even though God's law is good, it does not stop us from sinning. Instead, our sinfulness perverts God's law to sin even more.

We are powerless to stop sinning

So where does that leave us with our sin?

> For I do not do the good that I want to do, but I practice the evil that I do not want to do. Now if I do what I do not want, I am no longer the one that does it, but it is the sin that lives in me. So I discover this law: When I want to do what is good, evil is present with me. For in my inner self I delight in God's law, but I see a different law in the parts of my body, waging war against the law of my mind and taking me prisoner to the law of sin in the parts of my body.
>
> Romans 7:19-23

One of the ways we can recognise that God is the author of the Bible is by how accurately it describes the human condition. This passage is one of the many places God demonstrates how, as our creator, he understands us intimately.

This passage describes the struggle we all have. I cannot do the good I *want* to do but instead I do the evil I *don't* want to do. In my mind I can see that God's ways are good but, in my behaviour, I live for myself. We either all struggle in this way, or we give up the fight and embrace self-centred living. But none of us can defeat sin.

We all have such good intentions. We make New Year's resolutions, which are invariably broken by February. We set a goal of no more speeding fines, but cannot make it stick. We promise ourselves to never lose our temper again but cannot keep that until the end of the day.

All of us are powerless to stop sinning.

We may not like the idea, but we know it's true because we assume that, given the opportunity, we will choose to do wrong. It's why we lock the doors of our cars and houses. It's why the supermarkets video us at the self-checkout to ensure we do not steal the carrots. It's why we insist on contracts instead of handshakes. It's why legislators must work so hard to remove the loopholes from laws that we will try and exploit.

No matter how hard we try, our tendency is to act in our self-interest, and even at our best to do the evil we do not want to do.

> If we say, "We have no sin," we are deceiving ourselves, and
> the truth is not in us.
> If we say, "We have not sinned," we make him a liar,
> and his word is not in us.
>
> 1 John 1:8, 10

To claim to be sinless is not only self-deceptive but calls God a liar. For God has clearly informed us that all humans have sinned and continue to sin.

So, with the apostle Paul, we can only lament:

> What a wretched man I am! Who will rescue me from this
> body of death?
>
> Romans 7:24

God's good law condemns us

So, if God's law is powerless to save us, what is the purpose of his laws?

> No one will be justified in his sight by the works of the law,
> because the knowledge of sin comes through the law.
>
> Romans 3:20

The law operates as a standard for us against which to measure performance. However, because we are powerless to keep the law, it cannot save us. The result is that it only displays just how sinful we are

University courses commonly have entry requirements, including achieving a certain score in exams. The exams act as a benchmark against which to measure performance. Fail to reach the standard, and you will not be admitted.

God's law demands 100 percent obedience. It is a standard that our sinfulness makes impossible, so we all fail.

The apostle Paul said, this time in a letter to the Galatian Church:

> ...all who rely on the works of the law are under a curse, because it is written, Everyone who does not do everything written in the book of the law is cursed.
>
> Galatians 3:10

God does not grade on a curve, neither does he accept you if your good works outweigh your bad, nor is it about being better than anyone else. God's requirement is *absolute* obedience. And no one can do that. If you rely on observing God's laws to please him, Paul concludes, you will fail and be cursed.

Consider two houses standing side by side that are each structurally unsound. They are unsafe to live in so the building authorities declare them condemned. It does not matter that one has nicer interior walls, or light fittings, or more comfortable furnishings. In both cases their structure is rotten, and both must be demolished.

So too with us. One person might be kinder or more generous or harder working than another. But God is not comparing us with each other and selecting the top ten. We all stand condemned.

It does not matter how hard you try, how well you learn God's laws, how religious or devoted you are, none of us can escape the affliction of sin. And sin separates us from God.

> For all have sinned and fall short of the glory of God
>
> Romans 3:23

CHAPTER FIVE

What if I Fast and Pray?

Spiritual Discipline

Simeon, the Stylite, was a 5th century Christian in Asia Minor who lived perhaps the most famous life of 'asceticism' – one of severe discipline and self-denial – in an effort to please God. At the age of 13 he heard Matthew 5 (which we looked at in the last chapter) where Jesus declared that anyone seeking to please God, through obedience, would need to be perfect. From then on, he begged at the door of a monastery until he was admitted. There he refused food and drink for days and bound his body with tight cords until they cut deep into his flesh. The other monks considered his practices so extreme they expelled him.

Simeon then spent months in a hut, and then on a rocky outcrop, living as a hermit. But he still felt he lacked peace with God.

So, he journeyed to a remote area in Syria where he discovered a pillar (Greek word *Stylos* – hence Stylite). On this Simeon formed a one square metre platform on which he would spend the next 37 years. There he remained through cold, heat, rain and wind. Simeon reasoned that only by depriving himself of all physical comfort and pleasure could he ultimately conquer the power of sin in his life. He hoped that, if he withdrew from the surrounding world, he would not be tempted by what he might see or hear. He would stand for many hours meditating, praying, and teaching. Even during his final illness, he refused to leave the platform and there he died.

You cannot question Simeon's sincerity or his impressive self-discipline. He understood the seriousness of sin, and how it separated us from God. He determined that this knowledge should shape his whole life. He reasoned that closeness to God could only be achieved by his disciplined effort to withdraw from the distractions and comforts of the world. He therefore dedicated himself to ever increasing self-denial in pursuit of forgiveness from God.

Simeon was by no means the only one to go to such extreme lengths. Many other Stylites followed, living in the wilderness atop pillars. Others isolated themselves in caves, some whipped themselves, wore rough clothing, deprived themselves of food and sleep, and devoted themselves to memorising Scripture.

They endured any number of hardships and tortures, all in the hope that, as a result of their self-imposed sacrifices, they would somehow win favour with God. But no matter their efforts, you can see by the following quote that they failed to achieve any certainty of their worthiness before God.

> Suffer hunger, thirst, nakedness, be watchful and sorrowful; weep and groan in your heart; test yourselves, **to see if you are worthy of God**; despise the flesh, so that you may preserve your souls.
>
> Abba Anthony (Egyptian Desert Father, 251-356)
> (emphasis mine)

Many of us are also attracted by these examples of self-denial, and isolation from the world, as a means of drawing close to God. It seems to us that the world incites us to sin, so the less we interact with it the better for us. We reason that we will then have time to devote to prayer and fasting, and other religious practices, that will draw us closer to God. Many friends have explained to me how they have given up meat, or chocolate, or coffee, as a spiritual discipline. They hope that being able to forego those items will strengthen them to fight sin.

Ineffective Practices

So, what is God's assessment of these efforts at spiritual self-discipline? Do they help to combat sin and make someone worthy of him?

This is what the apostle Paul writes in his letter to the Colossian church in Asia Minor:

> If you died with Christ to the elements of this world, why do you live as if you still belonged to the world? Why do you submit to regulations: "Don't handle, don't taste, don't touch"? All these regulations refer to what is destined to perish by being used up; they are human commands and doctrines. Although these have a reputation for wisdom by promoting self-made religion, false humility, and severe treatment of the body, they are ***not of any value*** in curbing self-indulgence.
>
> Colossians 2:20-23
(emphasis mine)

Paul describes some, in the congregation at Colossae, who were living a life of self-denial. They had created rules to limit their enjoyment of pleasurable things: 'Don't handle, don't taste, don't touch'. They subjected their bodies to 'severe treatment'. Simeon would have felt right at home with them.

However, Paul concludes that, despite the extremity of their efforts that, "they are not of any value in curbing self-indulgence". This is a significant statement. No matter how restrictive or harshly you treat yourself it provides *no* benefit in controlling sin. None. Zero. Worthless.

It means that not even Simeon's radical self-denial was effective in producing spiritual progress. That is why, despite all the time he remained atop that pillar, and mourned his sin, and sought for holiness, Simeon never achieved the forgiveness and joy he so desperately desired.

In fact, the more he denied himself, the less worthy he felt, the further away God appeared, which only drove him to deny himself even more.

> The nearer a man comes to God, the more he sees himself to be a sinner.
>
> Mathois in *The Sayings of the Desert Fathers*

On one occasion, Simeon's mother asked to visit him. However, as he considered women a source of temptation, they were forbidden from being in his vicinity. From his pillar he sent word to her saying, "Do not disturb me now, my mother. *If* we become worthy, then we'll see each other in the next world." That 'if' is highly significant. After a lifetime of devotion, denying even contact with his mother, he could not be sure he had done enough. He had achieved no certainty that he would be found worthy of God; he had not merited spiritual peace.

In my own youth, when I would become conscious of my sin, I would pray until I felt I had expressed sufficient sorrow to be forgiven. The more I displeased God, the longer I would pray, but peace was hard to find. So

I would prostrate myself upon the ground while I prayed until I felt clean again. Longer and longer, and more intensely I would pray, driven by a lack of certainty that God, once again, found me acceptable.

I needed to hear the warning of the Apostle: self-denial is of *no* value in combatting sin.

Therefore, it didn't matter how many years Simeon sat on his pole, or how little he ate or slept. It does not matter how much we fast or pray, or what foods we forego, or even if we were to go and live on our own in a cave. None of it will not help us with combatting sin, none of it will not bring us closer to God, none of it can give us spiritual peace.

Manipulating God

Importantly in this passage Paul tells us why self-denial is spiritually impotent. It is because ascetism is a 'human command and doctrine' and a 'self-made religion' (verse 22-23). The latter is the word *ethelothreskia* (ἐθελοθρησκία) which is made from two root words. The first means 'the will', the choice-making, decision-making aspect of your mind, and the other root word means 'worship'. So, it means self-willed, human-determined worship of God. It is people making their own rules about what will be pleasing to God.

Imagine I borrowed your car. However, while I was reversing, I backed it into a fence leaving a small dent. Mortified at having damaged your vehicle, I decide to demonstrate the depth of my sorrow by running a marathon every day for a week. This would undoubtedly be a grand gesture. However, you had not requested it, nor is it related to the problem. This would be my solution to the issue, not yours. In fact, it would be difficult to see how you would be pleased by my effort as it would contribute nothing towards fixing the actual problem of the dent. My self-punishing response would be more about me, and my display of grief, than about you and addressing the damage I had done.

With self-denial it is not God who has suggested that, through it, we can somehow achieve forgiveness. This idea has been invented by us humans.

So why should we invent such a harsh system? What is so attractive about self-denial? We like it because it is a visible demonstration of spiritual depth and learning. Simeon attracted visitors from all over the world, from the lowly to the great and the good, to marvel at his devotion. They also came to glean his divine insights, for they assumed that God too would be impressed by his self-denial and reward him spiritually.

What attitude about God does this thinking reflect? It pictures God as reluctant to dispense his blessings unless forced by extreme displays of devotion. But this is simply an attempt to manipulate God. It is like the child who holds their breath until their parent allows them another biscuit, or the protestor who embarks on a hunger strike until the authorities agree to their demands.

This is the fatal flaw in the ascetic philosophy. This is not an approach to God to ask him for forgiveness. Instead, it is a desire to take matters into our own hands so that, by our personal merit, we might earn it. It is self-reliance on a self-made religion. It is 'autonomy' or running our lives our own way without God – and that is the very definition of sin. Asceticism is therefore the very opposite of reliance on God to provide for us, or of a desire to serve him.

An Evil Religion

But there is an even more sinister origin for such thinking that Paul explains in his letter to Timothy:

> Now the Spirit explicitly says that in later times some will depart from the faith, paying attention to deceitful spirits and the teachings of demons, through the hypocrisy of liars whose consciences are seared. They forbid marriage and demand abstinence from foods that God created to be received with gratitude by those who believe and know the truth.
>
> 1 Timothy 4:1-3

Paul reveals that the Holy Spirit condemns those who teach self-denial as the pathway to God. It deceives them into thinking they will achieve peace, whereas they become enslaved to ever increasing efforts to achieve the impossible. By relying on themselves rather than trusting in God, it causes them to 'depart from the faith'. No wonder the Spirit warns that, rather than being the way of God, asceticism is the teaching of demons.

This is a shocking statement.

Paul explains his reason in the next verse.

> For everything created by God is good, and nothing is to be rejected if it is received with thanksgiving...
>
> 1 Timothy 4:4

The Material World and its Creator are Good

Our universe is not an accident. It did not exist before God. It does not exist independently of him. God, by his own plan and design, made the entire universe from nothing.

Not only that but everything God made was completely *good*. God did not create a universe as a test or trap, or a series of temptations. At the end of every day of creation the book of Genesis records that God declared that all he had made was good. Then, on day 6 of creation, God made and designed human beings so that we might enjoy all of it, after which he concluded that his material universe was *very* good.

This helps us understand why Paul states that self-denial has no value in restraining sin. Creation is good, and sin is bad. Denying yourself that which is good is completely different to resisting temptation to do evil. Giving up ice cream may have its benefits, but it will not train you to stop lying.

Asceticism, however, takes the diametrically opposite view from God – which is always a dangerous position to take. It rejects the goodness of God's creation by considering it to be evil. It fails to accept God's good gifts and thank him for them.

Therefore, at best, asceticism is ingratitude towards God. It's the same ingratitude that the younger son displayed towards his generous father. It is the same ingratitude towards God that we noted characterises sin.

At worst, asceticism questions God's goodness in giving the material world to us. If we think the material world is evil, then what are we implying about the God who made it? From the very first temptation in the garden, Satan has seduced us to distrust God's benevolence. Doubting that God is good leads us to decide that we would be better off running life our own way – and that is at the heart of all sin. Asceticism is just such an attempt to create our own rules of right and wrong. And it fails because it's our way and not God's.

Asceticism draws us away from God

More fasting, more prayer, more withdrawal from the world is attractive to us because it offers us a way to merit our forgiveness. However, it drives us further away from God as it leads us to rely on ourselves and follow our own rules rather than turning us towards reliance on God.

It gives us false hope that if only we deny ourselves more or treat ourselves more harshly, we will find peace. Yet, self-denial has no value in making spiritual progress. We will only find ourselves making greater and greater efforts because we never feel we are worthy of God.

Where does that leave us?

So, what can we do? Sin has sentenced us to death. We are powerless to escape sin no matter what we do. We will fail, irrespective of how hard we try to be religious, or how much we discipline and deny ourselves. Therefore, how can we be restored to relationship with God, and rescued from sin and death?

What is the solution?

Thankfully, while salvation is impossible with man, 'with God all things are possible' (Matthew 19:26). We will see how God solves our sin problem in Part 2. There we are going to see that the solution all centres on why Jesus came.

PART 2

The Easter
Solution

CHAPTER SIX

Why did Jesus die?

What does Easter mean to you? For me it has always been the sights, sounds and smells of family, home and Church. It meant watching my mother making Tsoureki (Easter bread) – not to mention the overpowering goodness of its fresh-baked smell and eagerly devouring it with butter and honey. Then the Easter Sunday feast of roast lamb, which we shared with our extended family. The cracking of the eggs after lunch. The great crowd, candles in hand, that gathers at midnight for 'Great Saturday' when Jesus' resurrection is celebrated at Church.

Easter has always been the crowning festival in the Orthodox calendar and, for most of us, in our family's celebrations. This rightly reflects its central place in the Bible. Whilst the Christmas account features in only two Gospels, the cross of Jesus is reported extensively in all four Gospel biographies of Jesus – Matthew, Mark, Luke and John. In the remainder of the New Testament, Jesus' death and resurrection are central to understanding its message. These are the most significant events in history.

However, Easter is so familiar a celebration to us that it is easy to assume we know what it's all about. We know it's about Jesus' suffering, his death, and coming back to life. But have you ever asked yourself the simple question – Why? What was the purpose to it all that was so important that Jesus endured it? Arriving at an understanding of why Jesus had to die, and the significance of his rising to life, unlocks the meaning of Christianity and reveals the way to peace with God.

1. Jesus Did Not Need to Die

So why *did* Jesus die? On the surface this is a strange question to ask. After all, we expect everyone to die eventually, in one way or another. Yet God did not create us to die. In the Garden of Eden God created people to live forever, having provided for them the tree of life so they could have lived forever. However, Adam and Eve, the representatives of humankind, sinned by rebelling against God's rightful rule over them. The result was that they were expelled from the garden, and so cut-off from the tree of life. Outside of the garden they were sentenced to the existence in which we live now characterised by frustration, suffering and, importantly, death. God intended us to live forever and, only by our sin, must we now face death. As the apostle Paul writes, 'the wages of sin is death' (Romans 6:23).

However, Jesus is sinless. He did nothing deserving of death so was not required to face it. So why did *he* die?

Could it be that Jesus was simply another victim of circumstances, another unwilling casualty in an unjust world?

History is littered with the likes of Ghandi, Martin Luther King Jr, and Benazir Bhutto – all of whom, it could be argued, were assassinated as martyrs for good causes. Jesus could be considered the same as them. After all, Jesus threatened the status quo of the Jewish leadership. He challenged their teaching and authority and taught that God's Kingdom was near. This implied an end to both the Temple and Judaism. The New Testament makes clear that they had decided that Jesus had to die. The Roman governor, Pontius Pilate, was happy to oblige them, as he was facing pressure from his Emperor to appease the Judean locals. So there were strong political motives to remove a troublemaker like Jesus. And it was a common occurrence, for rebels against the Roman authorities, to be eliminated, like the two executed alongside Jesus. Was Jesus simply yet another crucified Judean Jew who had run afoul of the Roman government?

Jesus had also failed to meet the expectations of the populace. A popular teacher and miracle worker, Jesus was welcomed into Jerusalem by the crowds proclaiming him as the Messiah, which we commemorate on Palm Sunday. However, Jesus disappointed many who expected a Messiah to liberate them from Roman rule, and then re-establish an earthly Kingdom of Israel. So, within a week, the same crowds that welcomed him called for his crucifixion.

So, was Jesus merely another well-intentioned leader of a revolutionary movement who became a threat to the authorities, and who lost popularity, so succumbed to assassination? Was he just another historical figure who died for a just cause?

The answer is no. Jesus was never confused or confounded, or outsmarted. He repeatedly demonstrated his capacity to answer any question or accusation. He was never outmanoeuvred. He always remained in control in every situation. He cured diseases, expelled demons and, by raising people to life, demonstrated that he held ultimate power over life and death.[6]

Neither did the crowds control him. For when, on one occasion, a mob took Jesus towards a cliff with the intention of throwing him off, he merely

---

[6]   John 11:43-44, Mark 8:39-42, Luke 7:12-15

turned around and walked away through the crowd.[7] In that instance Jesus had determined that it was not his time. Jesus was always in control.

What about God, his Heavenly Father? Did God lose control? Again, the answer must be no.

The Father and his Son, Jesus, had been united for all eternity in love. God would not neglect to care for the life of Jesus. God cannot be caught off guard or tricked or surprised; he never looks away. He anticipates and rules over all events. God controls the political machinations of the powerful, and the thoughts of those in the crowds of Jerusalem. God is always in control of all things, from the smallest to the greatest.[8]

So, if Jesus did not deserve death, and neither Jesus nor God lost control, why then does Jesus die?

2. Jesus Chose to Die

We are left with only one possible explanation – that God's intention, right from the start, was for Jesus to die. This was God's plan from before creation, and the very purpose for which Jesus came to Earth[9]. Jesus understood this, and explained it clearly to his disciples on many occasions.[10]

> From then on Jesus began to point out to his disciples that
> it was necessary for him to go to Jerusalem and suffer many

---

[7]   Luke 4:29-30

[8]   Aren't two sparrows sold for a penny? Yet not one of them falls to the ground without your Father's consent. But even the hairs of your head have all been counted. So don't be afraid; you are worth more than many sparrows. Matthew 10:29-31

[9]   eg 1 Peter 1:20; Acts 2:23

[10] see also Matthew 17:22-23, 26:2; Mark 10:33-34; Luke 24:6-7; John 12:32-33

things from the elders, chief priests, and scribes, be killed, and be raised the third day.

Matthew 16:21

His disciples were always shocked to hear Jesus speak this way. Was Jesus not the Messiah, the Christ? Was he not God's anointed King whom he sent to rescue God's people? How would he be able to rule as a victorious King if he was executed? How could he rescue his people if he was dead? They thought that perhaps Jesus had misspoken or was feeling discouraged. Yet Jesus repeatedly asserted that the plan, from the beginning, was that he would die.

But the outspoken disciple, Peter, voiced the objections the others were thinking:

Peter took him (Jesus) aside and began to rebuke him, "Oh no, Lord! This will never happen to you!"

Matthew 16:22

"Stop all this negative talk Jesus," Peter was saying. "Snap out of it! You are God's chosen King. God would never allow you to be defeated by death."

To which Jesus responded,

"Get behind me, Satan! You are a hindrance to me because you're not thinking about God's concerns but human concerns."

Matthew 16:23

Jesus' rebuke of Peter indicates how important it is that Jesus must die. Jesus was describing the critical plan of God being worked out, at the centre of which was Jesus' death. To attempt to divert Jesus from the cross, as

Peter was suggesting, would be frustrating God's good plans – which was Satanic work.

Jesus is not merely saying it is likely that one day the authorities will stop me; nor that my enemies will inevitably kill me; nor that our movement may come to an end when, just like everyone else, I will eventually face death. Any other proponent of radical social change might concede the same.

Instead, Jesus had repeatedly insisted that his death was part of God's plan. His death was *intentional*. As we read in Matthew 16:21 above, Jesus says, "it was necessary" that he die. Jesus *must* die. He must die because that is the only solution to our sin problem, the only way we can be rescued from death.

3. Jesus Dies as Our Sin Substitute

We saw in Chapter Three that all of us have rebelled against God's rightful rule over us. As a result, we have cut ourselves off from the giver of life. The just punishment for our rebellion is death. Yet God declares that he takes no pleasure in condemning anyone, even though they deserve it.11 Instead, God longs to show mercy, to forgive people, to welcome them back into relationship and peace with him.

However, God is unswervingly just. Nothing escapes God's sight, and he will ensure that justice will be done against all who have done evil. Those who have exploited others, those who have murdered, the greedy, the liars, will all answer to God. All of them deserve punishment to fit their crimes. God cannot simply overlook evil and leave it unpunished. Were he to do so we could rightly exclaim that there is no justice in the universe. Evil would be perpetrated without consequences.

---

[11] Ezekiel 18:23

Justice is fundamental to God's character, and yet his deep desire is to show mercy. So how can God do both? How can God show mercy to people, and forgive them – yet remain just?

The only solution is for God to accept a substitute. Someone who will take our place and receive the punishment we deserve. That is why God the Son becomes a man. Being a man, he is a fitting substitute – one person dying in the place of other people. But, being also God, Jesus solves the problem of justice. Jesus is not an unsuspecting bystander whom God makes suffer for us, for that would create a new problem of injustice. Jesus is God himself. It is God, wanting to rescue us from sin and death, who takes upon himself the punishment we deserve.

> He himself bore our sins in his body on the tree; so that,
> having died to sins, we might live for righteousness. By his
> wounds you have been healed.
>
> 1 Peter 2:24

Jesus' death was not deserved by him, nor one in which he was overpowered by his opposition. Jesus willingly took our sin upon himself. He stood between us and God, and absorbed the righteous anger of God at our sin, and bore the wounds of death. He did it so we can be healed completely of the disease of sin which would otherwise have destroyed us.

From the very beginning Christians have understood that Christ died as a substitute for his people. Early Church Father, John Chrysostom, explained it like this:

> If one that was himself a king, beholding a robber and
> malefactor under punishment, gave his well-beloved son,
> his only-begotten and true, to be slain; and transferred the
> death and the guilt as well, from him to his son, (who was

himself of no such character) that he might both save the
condemned man and clear him from his evil reputation…

Commentary on 2 Corinthians 5:21

In 2006, a 21-year-old Australian woman, Kimberley Dear, on holidays
in the US state of Missouri, booked in for a tandem skydive. However,
soon after take-off, the plane suffered a catastrophic engine failure. When
the experienced skydiver, 22-year-old Robert Cook, realised the aircraft
was going to crash, he grabbed Kimberley, calmly spoke to her, and told
her to prepare herself. As they were already in harnesses for their tandem
jump, Robert clipped them together. While the plane was descending, he
put his arms around her and pulled her close, cushioning her head on his
shoulders. He said to her: "When the plane is about to hit the ground,
make sure you're on top of me so that I'll take the force of the impact".
When the plane struck the ground Robert absorbed the full energy of the
collision and died. Kimberley survived because Robert had positioned himself between the threat of death, and her. He sacrificed his life for her. He
died so she would not.

Kimberley's father said: "He met Kimberley, as far as I know, that day.
I would do that for her, but I can't believe that a stranger who just met her
would knowingly give up his life for her."[12]

In his death Jesus gave his life for us. Knowingly, planned, and intentional. He knew our desperate need, that we would not survive God's
judgement, so he took our place to face it for us.

---

[12] https://www.smh.com.au/national/skydivers-bravery-saves-aussies-life-20060
802-gdo3b1.html

"You the sinless One, were numbered amongst the
transgressors, in order to save mankind,
O Most Forbearing Lord, glory to You."
Liturgy of Holy Thursday Evening

4. Jesus Died to Substitute for Many

But Jesus dies, not for just for one person but for as many as come to him
for forgiveness:

> For even the Son of Man did not come to be served, but to
> serve, and to give his life as a ransom for many.
>
> Mark 10:45

We are familiar with the concept of ransoms. In situations where someone is kidnapped, or taken hostage or captured in war, it is not uncommon
for a payment to be demanded before the captive is freed. Sometimes it is
money. On other occasions it is a hostage swap – people are exchanged for
people.

Jesus states that his very purpose is to ransom those who are held captive
to death by taking their place. It would make sense that the one perfect
man could swap with one other person and take their capital punishment
for them. Yet Jesus is claiming that he can swap his life to liberate the lives
of *many*. How can Jesus take the place of more than one person?

In 2006, an Israeli soldier, Gilad Shalit, was captured by Hamas mil-
itants during an attack. As the months dragged on, there was a massive
public campaign in Israel to secure Shalit's release. His family led a highly
visible and persistent campaign, including marches, protests, and a permanent tent outside the Prime Minister's residence. Extensive media coverage
kept him in the public eye. Additionally, the Israeli government was acutely

aware of the psychological impact on Israeli soldiers, and their families, if there was any perception that they failed to protect their own. The 'Gilad Shalit' campaign garnered widespread public support, putting significant pressure on the Israeli government to secure his release. His freedom became a highly valuable outcome.

In 2011, after intense and prolonged negotiations, and five years of captivity, Shalit was freed in exchange for 1027 Palestinian and Arab-Israeli prisoners. Over that time Shalit had acquired such value that the Israeli government, and Hamas, agreed that this one man's liberty was worth that of over a thousand others.

Shalit was, of course, highly valued by his family and his community. But he was only one man, worth the same as any other person, for every human life has the same value, that of being made in the image of God. But Shalit's value was inflated out of political expediency. The power brokers who negotiated his release assessed his political value to the government of Israel, especially the impact on their prospects of re-election. Their resulting calculation meant he could be exchanged for many.

The value of Jesus' life is not a result of publicity, or of being loved by many, or the product of an arbitrary or political calculation. The value of Jesus' life arises from the inherent worth of his being. Jesus is more than a man – he is God become flesh. His life is not only more valuable than just one, or even many human lives – the life of God become man is intrinsically of *infinite* worth. That is how Jesus can be the substitute for many. That's how he can promise that "Everyone the Father gives me will come to me, and the one who comes to me I will never cast out" (John 6:37). Jesus' life can substitute for all, and for anyone who comes to him.

Jesus' life is of such great value that he takes upon himself *all* of the judgement that his people deserve. For them there is no more death left to die. There is no more penalty of sin left to answer for. There is no sin so great that Jesus' death cannot pay the price of it; there is no sin so small that Jesus, through his death, has overlooked forgiving it.

Those who accept the ransom that Jesus offers can be certain that they are fully forgiven. Not because they deserve it, or are less sinful, or any better, than anyone else. But instead, on the basis that the value of Jesus' life is sufficient to pay the ransom price completely and set his people free.

> For what else was able to cover our sins except the righteousness of that one? In whom was it possible for us, the lawless and ungodly to be justified except in the Son of God alone? O the sweet exchange, O the inscrutable work, O the unexpected benefits, that the lawlessness of many might be hidden in one righteous man, while the righteousness of one might justify many lawless men.
>
> *Epistle of Mathetes to Diognetus* 9:3-5 (c 130-160 AD)

5. Jesus died because He loves us

But why does Jesus do this for us? We are not good; we are sinners. We have all turned our back on God and rebelled against his rightful rule over us. Like the younger son in the story Jesus told (Chapter 3) we wish God did not exist, no longer there making demands on our lives. No longer telling us how to live. We have made a mess of the universe God loves – of ourselves, of one another, and of the world. Why would Jesus want to rescue us from death?

Picture an arsonist who has repeatedly lit fires that led to people's deaths. Family houses, schools, nursing homes. Someone who delights in watching the flames, and the power they have over other's lives. Such a person deserves to be brought to justice, and face punishment for their crimes.

Imagine there was a firefighter, whose job was to extinguish those fires as well as discover and identify the bodies left behind. They would rightly be disgusted by the arsonist's destruction of lives and property. They would recognise the need to bring such a person to justice.

Suppose the day came when that arsonist found themselves trapped in a fire of their own making, their life in immediate danger. Confronting the scene, the firefighter is faced with a challenge – should they risk their own life to save this arsonist? Here is someone who has been responsible for the deaths of many others. They are now being faced with the consequences of their actions. The arsonist can blame no-one but themselves for their own death.

It is possible that the firefighter would risk their life to save someone like this. It is the kind of profession where life is valued, and rescuing others is what they are trained to do. But, what if rather than simply rescuing them, they were asked to swap places with the arsonist – to face the certain fiery death that the arsonist has brought upon themselves. And that the result of that exchange would be that the arsonist can go free, facing no consequences for destroying lives and property. It would be the firefighter facing the justice that the arsonist deserved. Such a scenario is unimaginable.

Yet this is what Jesus does.

> For rarely will someone die for a just person – though for a good person perhaps someone might even dare to die. But God proves his own love for us in that while we were still sinners, Christ died for us.
>
> …while we were enemies, we were reconciled to God through the death of his Son…
>
> Romans 5:7-8,10

We have not earned forgiveness. We cannot repay the price of our lives back to God. We deserve nothing from God but his anger. It is not because God sees some merit in us, neither does he reward our effort, or good intentions, by 'helping those who help themselves'. Sin makes us God's *enemies*, not his friends.

And Jesus is aware more than anyone how much our sinful lives deserve judgement before God. Yet, Jesus willingly takes our place, for us he faces the white-hot inferno that is the righteous anger of God, even though he knows it means certain death for him.

So why does Jesus die for us? You can see it above in verse 8. It is the ultimate proof of God's love for us. In light of God's absolute certainty that all of us deserve eternal destruction, the Cross of Christ displays his overwhelming compassion for us. Even though we are his enemies, yet Jesus loves us so profoundly that he is willing to spend his priceless life to secure our salvation.

It also demonstrates God's conviction that there is no other way for us to be saved. For if we could rescue ourselves by obeying the law, or through self-denial, or through religious effort, why would God have paid for us such a great price as the sacrifice of his son (Galatians 2:21)?

> For in your merciful compassion, Master, you could not bear to see the human race under the tyranny of the Devil, but came and saved us.
> *Service of Holy Baptism*[13]

---

[13] in *Holy Baptism* St Andrews Orthodox Press Sydney 2008 p45

6. Did Jesus' Death do Enough?

For us who are helpless, and otherwise hopeless, in the face of God's judgement, this is amazing news. For it gives us the assurance of God's promise to us when he says:

> For God loved the world in this way: he gave his one and only son, so **that everyone who believes in him will not perish but have eternal life.**
>
> John 3:16
> (emphasis mine)

And once more:

> He erased the certificate of debt, with its obligations, that was against us and opposed to us, and has taken it away by nailing it to the cross.
>
> Colossians 2:14

The death of Jesus, in our place, removes all our sin and the debt of death we owe to God. Everyone who accepts Jesus' death in their place is reconciled to God and has received eternal life. No more are we enemies, but now friends. No longer at war, but at peace. We can be completely forgiven because Jesus has taken the punishment we deserve. In these words, God himself, who does not lie, has assured us of this.

Do you believe God's words? Do you think Jesus did enough in his death to pay for your sins, and of everybody who comes to him? The answer to both questions should be YES. It does not matter what you have done in your life – nothing is beyond the forgiveness that Jesus brings. For Jesus' life is of such immense value that nothing is lacking from the price he paid for us, nothing needs to be added, nothing depends on us.

There is no need to supplement the price that Jesus paid to ransom his people from sin. In fact, to suggest we need to contribute to our forgiveness questions the value of Jesus' sacrifice, the worth of his life.

> "Christ is the new Pascha, the sacrificial Victim, the Lamb of God **that takes away the sin of the world.**"
> "**No one need grieve over sins**; forgiveness has dawned from the tomb."
>
> *Orthros of the Resurrection* (First liturgy of Easter Sunday)

Jesus offers the deal of – not just this lifetime – but of eternity as well. He offers to take our sinfulness, and death, for his holiness and life. We know his offer is genuine. If we accept it, we will discover absolute joy, deep relief, and genuine certainty of eternal life.

Why would we pass up this offer?

JACKY'S STORY

My name is Jacky, I am 61, a dentist and mother of 3.

I was raised in a typical Greek Orthodox family. Mum was the enthusiastic churchgoer who would take us to all the Church festivals, baptisms, weddings, funerals, memorials, and Greek school. Dad was the worker who respected the priest and the Church, but kept his distance.

We were – and remain to this day – close friends with the priest and his family. Largely because of this close association, I had always thought of myself as a Christian. However, in university I met another student who offered to start reading the Bible with me. We looked at the Gospel of John and, the more I read, the more questions I had.

I went back to my priest and asked why he didn't encourage us to read the Bible. He told me that the scriptures were holy and needed the priests to interpret them for us. However, as I kept on reading, the Bible's message seemed to be so clear. I knew God was speaking to me in the Bible and understood that it was true. And after all, I thought, why would God have caused it to be written if he didn't want us to understand him?

It finally dawned on me that I had never understood why Jesus had to die on the cross. I knew about all the Easter events we celebrated in Church that Jesus had died for my sins, but it had never been personal for me. But now I could see that Jesus taking my sins away made a relationship with God possible.

In Orthodoxy I was going through the motions, keeping the rules, and driven to obedience by shame. But when I decided to follow Jesus, I knew that the blood of Christ created the way for me to ask for the forgiveness of God. I was freed from guilt and shame because I could now give my sin to God and have a clean slate.

My parents, however, did not greet my decision with joy, and years of heated discussion followed. However, as his end approached, my father started asking questions. I assured him with the words of Jesus, that whoever believes in him shall not perish but will be given eternal life. He said to me: "I have been the god of my own life, and I am not worthy of God's forgiveness". But we looked at Matthew 20 to understand that, in the kingdom of Heaven, God in his generosity grants all who come to him eternal life, whether they come at the beginning or at their very last opportunity. After that we prayed together, where my father asked God for his forgiveness and, in his relief, cried tears of joy. He died the next day.

The best thing about this new life in Christ is having the sure hope of being with Jesus in Heaven. I'm looking forward to being united with my father, and my brothers and sisters in Christ who, with me, will be transformed into the likeness of Christ. There we will sing songs of joy and be freed from suffering. My deepest longing is for the remainder of my family and children to also know that joy now, and that hope for the future.

CHAPTER SEVEN

The Once for All Sacrifice

For Christ also suffered for sins once for all, the righteous for the unrighteous,
that he might bring you to God.
1 Peter 3:18

In the previous chapter we saw that the reason that Jesus died was to give his life to ransom many from sin. However, how did he take the place of his people? People die every day. Ordinary people, Kings, Queens, Presidents, and even religious leaders. However, none of their deaths achieve anything for anyone else. How is it that Jesus' death can be of benefit to us?

To answer that question, we need to consider the religion of the Old Testament people of God, the Israelites.

Life for life

Around 2,000 years before Christ, God spoke to Abraham, declaring that he and his descendants would be blessed, and also that all people on Earth would be blessed through them. Abraham's descendants were the people of Israel. That is why Jesus was sent to be born an Israelite for, through Jesus the son of Abraham, God's blessing of salvation comes to all the peoples of the world.

The Israelites were therefore God's special people. God would be with them and bless them as long as they continued to serve him.

However, the Israelites were sinful people. Like all people everywhere they continually fractured their relationship with God by rebelling against him, and failing to obey him.

So, to deal with their sin, God instructed the Israelites to build a special meeting place that would eventually become the building called the Temple in Jerusalem. It was from here that God was present in the centre of his people. In the Temple, the people of Israel could approach God to make peace with him.

However, how could they approach God when they were sinful, unforgiven, knowing that sin deserves death? In the Temple, God provided the solution – animals would be sacrificed in their place.

> According to the Law almost everything is purified with blood, and without the shedding of blood there is no forgiveness.
>
> Hebrews 9:22

Money, crops, goods – nothing else was an acceptable substitute. Life had been forfeited so a life must be paid. So, instead of the person, it is the animal which loses its life.

Therefore, everyday Israel's priests would need to offer animals before God in the Holy Place in the Temple. It was necessary every day because, just like us, the sin of the people of Israel was never ending, and constantly needed forgiveness.

The Day of Atonement

However, once a year there was a special sacrifice. On that day, the Day of Atonement (or Yom Kippur as it is called today), the High Priest would go beyond the Holy Place where regular offerings were made, and enter through a curtain into the *Most* Holy Place. Inside was the symbolic throne of God. Before God, this Priest would sacrifice a bull and a goat for the sins of the entire people of Israel. In this action God's judgement would be turned away from his people, and onto the animals being sacrificed. This would make 'atonement' for the sins of Israel, restoring their relationship with God.

One year later, the Day of Atonement, with its sacrifice, would be repeated. And again, the following year. And the following year, and the next, and the year after that. But this yearly recurrence of the same sacrifices only demonstrated how ineffective they were.

> Since the law has only a shadow of the good things to come, and not the reality itself of those things, it can never perfect the worshipers by the same sacrifices they continually offer year after year. Otherwise, wouldn't they have stopped being offered, since the worshippers, purified once and for all, would no longer have any consciousness of sins? But in the sacrifices there is a reminder of sins year after year.
>
> Hebrews 10:1-3

As the writer to the Hebrews points out, if their sins had been permanently forgiven by them there would be no need to return. In fact, their very repetition reminds them that their sins remained.

But the writer points out another reason why these sacrifices were an inadequate substitute.

For it is impossible for the blood of bulls and goats to take
away sins.

Hebrews 10:4

If I was sentenced to gaol, I might request that another person could
take my place, and serve my sentence for me. Even though the court would
rightly insist I should be punished for my own crime, at least I could argue
that the exchange would be human for human – like for like.

However, what if I suggested my dog take my place in gaol? (Don't
worry – he sleeps all day anyway and would probably get more exercise
there.) The judge would rightly mock my suggestion. Love my dog as
much as I do, humans and animals are of a qualitatively different order. We
are not an equivalent swap for one another.

The lives of bulls and goats on the day of Atonement can never substitute for those of humans. No matter how many times they are offered, they
will not pay for sins.

A Copy of the Heavenly Temple

Yet this was the religion established under God's direct and exacting
instructions. If any system should be successful in reconciling people to
God, it should be this one. But it did not matter how meticulously the
Jewish people offered their sacrifices, observed all the laws and restrictions,
and celebrated all the required festivals. Not even the religious structure
given by God himself could reconcile people to him.

So, what was God's purpose in establishing such a system?

It served as an earthly 'copy and shadow of the heavenly things' (Hebrews
8:5). The very function of the Temple, with its priests and sacrifices, was to
point to a greater reality.

Like many others, as a child I constructed many Airfix kits – model planes, ships, tanks. All of them were scaled down facsimiles of the original. As faithful copies, I could look at them and see the details of the actual object. One day, when I saw the real thing, I could recognise it and identify the details that were reproduced in the model. However, it would be a mistake to expect my 1/76 polystyrene Sherman tank to fire a 75mm shell, or to offer any protection in the event of an armed invasion.

The earthly Temple was a model in the same way. It functioned to prepare the world and direct our attention so that, when Christ arrived, we could recognise him and understand what he came to do. But it could never function in the way the real heavenly Temple did before God. The earthly Temple was a model of what people needed to have their sins forgiven – they needed a life sacrifice to be brought before God. But animal sacrifices were never intended to achieve forgiveness. Instead, their very purpose was to point us to the *effective* sacrifice of Christ.

An effective sacrifice

> But Christ has appeared as a high priest of the good things that have come. In the greater and more perfect tabernacle not made with hands (that is, not of this creation), he entered the most holy place once for all time, not by the blood of goats and calves, but by his own blood, having obtained eternal redemption.
>
> Hebrews 9:11-12

Jesus' work was not to offer a sacrifice in the Temple in Jerusalem. He appears before God face-to-face in the real heavenly Most Holy Place.

Neither does he bring the ineffective sacrifice of animals. Instead, he offers his own life and, with it, he redeems the people of God.

To redeem is like paying the ransom we considered in the last chapter. It means to purchase someone out of bondage or obligation. The word redeem was used in the context of slavery to describe paying the price to secure a slave's freedom.

The Perfect Once for All Time Sacrifice

As we saw in the last chapter, the value of Jesus' sacrifice is so great that with it he buys back God's people *eternally*. It means that, unlike the animal sacrifices, his does not need to be repeated. His forgiveness also lasts forever. Jesus' sacrifice is once *for all time*.

But there is another way in which this is a 'once for all' sacrifice

> Every priest stands day after day ministering and offering the same sacrifices time after time, which can never take away sins. But this man, after offering **one sacrifice for sins forever**, sat down at the right hand of God. He is now waiting until his enemies are made his footstool. For by one offering he has **perfected forever** those who are sanctified.
>
> Hebrews 10:11-14
>
> (emphasis mine)

Jesus' one sacrifice completely removes *all* the sins of *all* his people. No further sacrifices are required, nothing needs to be added, nothing more needs to be done. Jesus has achieved the perfection of his people. His work is complete. The sacrifice Jesus brings is made once *for all sin*.

Once for all time – once for all sin. Jesus offers complete and perfect forgiveness.

Childhood leukaemia is a devastating illness. It is a terrible burden for the still growing child, and the parents who love them. However, while as recently as the 1960s it was uniformly fatal, but now there are a broad range of effective treatments. Now over 90 percent of treated children go into remission – the illness fades into the background. More significantly, most children with leukaemia are actually cured!

Cure is one better than remission. It means not just the slowing of the illness, and not even merely a postponement of death. A cure means these children will live just as long as those of the same age who *never had* leukaemia. It will be as if they never suffered from this cancer.

It is such a wonderful benefit of modern medicine that someone can contract such a vicious disease process as leukaemia – while they are still growing – but then to have it combated so effectively that it has no long-term consequences on their physical health. It is astounding that such a reversal could be possible.

Yet what Jesus accomplished in his death is even greater. For sin is a disease that kills everyone affected by it – and that is every human being. Sin is a guarantee of spiritual death before God. Yet the intervention of Jesus, the application of his sacrifice to a person, will produce a definitive cure. They receive a total spiritual cleansing. So conclusive a cure for sin that it never has to be done again. So complete that it grants to the sinner a life with God as if they had never sinned.

No one else but the Saviour himself, who at the beginning made everything himself out of nothing, could bring the corrupted to incorruption, for no one else but the image of the Father could recreate men in God's image; no one else could make the mortal immortal ... Since the debt owed by all men had to be paid (for all men had to die), he came among us. After he had demonstrated his deity by his works, he offered his sacrifice on behalf of all and surrendered his temple (body) to death in the place of all men.

Athanasius of Alexandria

On the Incarnation of the Word (d AD 373)

Grasping this truth will truly set you free. You do not have to depend on your performance, your spiritual effort, your self-denial, or your religiosity. These will not, and cannot, liberate you from sin. Only Jesus can do this *for* us. When he applies his sacrifice to our account we will be cleansed from sin and perfected for all eternity. At peace with God. Prepared to meet him without shame.

In the last chapter we saw that the value of Jesus life can ransom us completely from judgement. In this chapter we have seen how the quality of Jesus sacrifice means we can be forgiven for all time.

In the next chapter we are going to consider how Jesus can apply his ransom and sacrifice for us before God.

ANASTASIA'S STORY

My name is Anastasia. I am 51, recently divorced and a mother to two children. I work as an Orthotist in Sydney, Australia.

For as long as I can remember I have longed to know God. My local Greek Orthodox Church rightly taught me that God was to be feared and revered. I understood that my sin kept me separated from God – but I was not taught, and did not know, how to make that right.

I was very conscious of my sin and knew that it meant I did not deserve God's favour. I remember waking in the morning and praying that I would not commit any sins that day. But every day I would fail even to keep all the 10 commandments, let alone the remainder of God's laws. I knew that Jesus had said that, if your eye causes you to sin, you should pluck it out to save yourself from hellfire (Matthew 18:9). That worried me greatly for, if I had to take such extreme measures against sin, I knew I would no longer be able to live. Surely, I thought, God did not want that for me.

Then, when I was 16, a friend of mine at school told me Jesus could be my friend and pointed me to the Bible. I could see that the Bible was not just a book to be kissed, but which contained the answers from God that I needed. I started to read a Bible on my own, but I didn't know where to begin. However, at 18 when I started university, I joined a Bible study group and finally began to understand. I felt so unworthy and wanted assurance that I could be a true Christian.

My answer came when I read Galatians 2:21

> I do not set aside the grace of God, for if righteousness
> comes through the law, then Christ died for nothing.

Suddenly I understood that Jesus had died willingly to solve the human problem of sin. If I denied it, I would be treating his death on the cross as

useless, and without power. I always knew my name meant 'Resurrection' in Greek and now, for the first time, I embodied my name's true meaning: Christ came to liberate our souls from guilt and death and to give us new life.

I now knew the privilege of being able to approach God directly through Jesus as my high priest. God started, and continues now, to change my heart and mind to become more like him.

Later, when I was rejected and betrayed in my marriage, I came to understand a snippet of what Christ went through for mankind. Even though Jesus was hated by the world, his only desire was to return good to us by giving us the forgiveness we could never deserve. Healing from my divorce was so much easier knowing that God truly understands me, has made me, and has lived with me through all of the emotions I have experienced. What an amazing Father and God we have!

CHAPTER EIGHT

The Eternal Priest

Visiting a Monarch

I have a friend who was once granted a private audience with Queen Elizabeth II. However, he was not allowed to just walk up to the front door of Balmoral Castle and knock. Thorough and strict rules of protocol were communicated to him and needed to be observed – when to speak, what to say and do, what not to say or do, and how to address Her Majesty. Security checks were performed on him to make sure there was nothing unacceptable in his past. Guards were present on the day, both visible and hidden.

Importantly he was there because he was invited, not because he took it on himself to turn up. He was recommended by another. He was accompanied into her presence.

My understanding is that Queen Elizabeth was always a gracious and forgiving host to her guests. Never once did she send anyone to the Tower of London, let alone remove their head for breaking protocol. When one of our Prime Ministers placed a hand on her back to guide her during a visit, the worst outcome he suffered was condemnation by the media. Yet

even without the threat of significant consequences, I have no doubt that visiting someone, who is so set apart from ordinary people, would be a nerve-wracking experience.

God is no mere earthly monarch. He is separated from us by being outside of creation by virtue of being its maker. He is also distinct from us by being entirely good. It is a complete otherness from us, and specialness, that is what is meant by the Biblical word 'Holy'. The holiness of God refers to the absolute moral purity of God, and the absolute moral distance between God and his human creatures.

God is also all-powerful and unwaveringly just. As we saw in Chapter Six, he cannot simply ignore evil or tolerate sin. He cares for his creation, and us his creatures, and will not allow any injustice against them to remain unpunished. We cannot simply turn up to him while we remain guilty of sin.

The Old Testament prophet Isaiah had a vision in which he sees God seated in his glory on his heavenly throne. Isaiah notices that the angels cover their faces with their wings, as even those heavenly beings cannot bear to look upon the moral purity of God. When this scene appears before Isaiah he exclaims:

> Woe is me for I am ruined
> because I am a man of unclean lips
> and live among a people of unclean lips,
> and because my eyes have seen the King,
> the Lord of Armies.
>
> Isaiah 6:5

Isaiah understands that no one can simply walk up to God and be found acceptable. He recognises the unbreachable gap of holiness between God and himself. He cries out, in the expectation of his destruction, in the face of the just judge God.

The Most Holy Place

In the last chapter I wrote about the Temple religion instituted by God. The Temple stood in the centre of capital Jerusalem, and in the centre of Israel's religious life, so was a reminder of how close God was to them. In the Temple was his symbolic dwelling place – there was his throne, from there He ruled over Israel, and from there he could be accessed.

Simultaneously, however, the Temple reminded Israel of how far away they were from God. For ordinary Israelites could not simply walk in at any time. Because of their sin they had to keep their distance from God. Only priests could enter the Holy Place, and only then with sacrifices for sin. But they were not permitted to enter the Most Holy Place and come face to face with God. Only the *High* Priest could enter there, once a year on the Day of Atonement. Even then only after offering a sacrifice for his own sin, for he too was unacceptable to God and needed to be cleaned. No-one else could approach God that closely. In fact, the High Priest would always enter with a rope tied around his waist. This was in case he died while in the Most Holy Place, as no one would be permitted to enter to retrieve his body – they would have to pull him out.

God was right there amongst them – and yet sin created a gulf between the Israelites and God. And, as we saw in the last chapter, the blood of bulls and goats was ineffective at forgiving sin. They could not bridge that gulf. Israel had to keep their distance.

This remains a problem for us all. We cannot simply walk in on God. How do we approach God in order to be at peace with him, and relate to him?

We need a mediator. Someone who can represent us. A priest who stands between us and God.

Israel had plenty of priests and High Priests. But there are several problems with relying on human priests.

All Human Priests Die

In common with everyone, priests share the problem of death.

> Now many have become Levitical priests, since they are prevented by death from remaining in office.
>
> Hebrews 7:23

God had designated the descendants of Levi to be the priests who served his people of Israel in the Temple. As they died, they were replaced by their sons, who were then succeeded by theirs, and so on. There needed to be a steady supply of replacements, because all of them would eventually succumb to death.

This is a problem if we rely on these priests to intercede between us and God. For their intercession eventually ends. But we keep on sinning. How can we be certain of eternal forgiveness if the efforts of these priests are only temporary?

All Human Priests are Imperfect

Also, in common with all humanity, priests are sinful. In other words, we are looking to them to provide us with a solution to a problem they are powerless to solve for themselves.

Their sin means they do not have guaranteed access to God. The Old Testament priests needed to conduct sacrifices to cleanse themselves before they could approach God to sacrifice for the people. And this cleaning was only temporary, for they would certainly sin again and require another sacrifice for themselves.

But not only does this limit their access to God, but the sinfulness of human priests also means they cannot be completely trusted. Like all of us, they are swayed by self-centredness; they will not always fulfil their duties, and they will fail in serving us.

All Human Priests are Earthbound

The Old Testament priests were also limited to serve in the earthly Temple, which was only ever a 'copy and shadow of the heavenly things' (Hebrews 8:5). The purpose of the sacrifices that occurred there were to point ahead to a better sacrifice to be applied in Heaven. Of course, human priests have no access to the heavenly realms. They could not approach God and offer sacrifices directly before him.

All Human Priests are Ineffective

This one is the most critical: human priests cannot make any progress against sin.

> Every priest stands day after day ministering and offering
> the same sacrifices time after time, which can never take
> away sins.
>
> Hebrews 10:11

As we saw in the previous chapter, even the Israelite system of sacrifices, established by God, could not secure forgiveness for people. Neither then can many prayers spoken, or liturgies conducted, or Holy Communions received. It does not matter how sincere, or devout, or caring, is the priest who offers them is; these offerings to God are powerless to forgive.

Only one sacrifice is acceptable to God, and only one priest can offer it.

The High Priest we Need

> For this is the kind of high priest we need: holy, innocent, undefiled, separated from sinners, and exalted above the heavens. He doesn't need to offer sacrifices every day, as high priests do – first for their own sins, then for those of the people. He did this once for all time when he offered himself.
>
> Hebrews 7:26-27

Jesus Christ is the High Priest we all need.

Jesus is sinless and holy. He is always acceptable to approach his Heavenly Father on our behalf. He can advocate for us alone before God, as he does not need to protect himself from God's wrath at the same time.

Jesus is our priest – the only priest – in the heavenly realms. Because Jesus is there, he can offer his sacrifice in the one place that counts – directly before God (Hebrews 8:1-2).

During 2021 we were searching for a new home interstate. We could see various houses online, but we did not know much about any of the areas in which the houses were located. Plus, there was another rather significant problem. We were in Covid lockdown. We could not travel to see and consider any houses or negotiate a sale.

The solution for us was to engage a buyer's advocate who worked in that city. We could not go there, so she acted as our representative. She was familiar with the areas in which we were looking and could advise us of the pros and cons of each one. She was able to view the houses in which we were interested. She knew what we should pay for the houses, and knew all the Real Estate agents, so could negotiate the best price for us. She made the payment and finalised the sale.

She was there when we could not be. And, importantly, she had the expertise which we lacked. She advocated on our behalf, in our interests.

Jesus advocates like this for his people before his heavenly Father. He is our representative, negotiating on our behalf. No one else can do this for us – only Jesus is qualified. He knows the price that must be paid, and offers the perfect and completely acceptable sacrifice of himself. His is the only sacrifice that can secure forgiveness for his people.

> He that is our advocate, is the Lord of all, and God the Father is more ready to give than we to ask; he desires our salvation more than we ourselves do; and his will is, that all men should be saved.
>
> St. John Chrysostom
> (c. 347–407) *Homilies on the Gospel of Matthew*

Jesus Intercedes for us Forever

> But because he remains forever, he holds his priesthood permanently. Therefore, he is able **to save completely** those who come to God through him, since he always lives to intercede for them.
>
> Hebrews 7:24-25
> (emphasis mine)

Finally, our High Priest Jesus lives forever. He will always intercede for us; he will always stand before God on behalf of his people to ensure his sacrifice is applied to them.

Jesus is holy, forever alive and present in Heaven, to eternally stand between us and God. He presents before God the perfect sacrifice, sufficient to pay for all our sins. That is why this God-inspired text of Hebrews can declare that Jesus saves his people *completely*. For our great High Priest, Jesus, lives to apply his sacrifice for our sin forever.

Jesus needs no help

Also, because Jesus' work is complete, he requires no help in interceding for us. He does not need the assistance of heavenly saints or earthly priests.

> For there is one God and one mediator between God and
> mankind, the man Christ Jesus
>
> 1 Timothy 2:5

Jesus is the one, final, perfect priest appointed by God. His mediation is perfect and sufficient. God welcomes those who approach him through Jesus.

Nothing else needs to be done. Guaranteed peace with God. What a great High Priest is Jesus.

God has truly demonstrated his love for us in these comforting words. He could simply have told us we were forgiven in Christ. However, he has patiently explained to us how he has achieved forgiveness in order to provide us with even more assurance. God does not want us to fear the future when we come before him, but wants to reassure us that Christ has done all that is required to save us *completely*.

> For though he is the son of God and shares the same nature as he that begot him, yet he became our mediator and intercessor, and he holds communion with the father, asking on our behalf what is profitable for our salvation.
>
> St. Cyril of Alexandria (c. 376–444) *Commentary on the Gospel of John*

Welcomed into the presence of God

Remember, at the beginning of this chapter, the prophet Isaiah had a vision of God on his throne, at which he lamented that he would be destroyed. At that instant,

> ...one of the seraphim flew to me, and in his hand was a glowing coal that he had taken from the altar with tongs. He touched my mouth with it and said:
>
> Now that this has touched your lips,
> your iniquity is removed
> and your sin is atoned for.
>
> Isaiah 6:6-7

Isaiah could only escape judgement, approach God and speak with him once his sins were forgiven by a heavenly sacrifice.

So on what basis do we think God should welcome us and hear our prayers?

Returning to Queen Elizabeth, you could not just walk into her office or lounge room and ask her a favour. If you wrote to her, you would receive a polite answer from one of her secretaries. Not only could the Queen not physically read all the letters she received, quite frankly, you and I are not important enough for our letter to merit her attention.

Of course, God is all-hearing and all-seeing so can hear our prayers. However, as we have seen, sin separates us from God. We have turned our back on God, rejected him as our Heavenly Father. Why would we be so arrogant as to assume that God must listen to us when we need something from him? Why would we assume we deserve to be heard, or answered by him, or have our requests granted?

Like Isaiah, only when our sins are forgiven is it possible to approach God in prayer. And this access to God is what Jesus accomplishes through his sacrifice. Only then do we have the one mediator through whom we can approach God.

> Therefore, brothers and sisters, since we have boldness to enter the sanctuary through the blood of Jesus – he has inaugurated for us a new and living way through the curtain (that is, through his flesh) – and since we have a great high priest over the house of God, **let us draw near with a true heart in full assurance of faith**
>
> Hebrews 10:19-22

Jesus, our High Priest, has cleaned us completely, rendering us acceptable to God. We no longer have to fear approaching God like Isaiah. Now forgiven, we are invited to approach God *boldly*, sure that God will find us acceptable and welcome us into his presence. We can approach God in prayer and be confident on the day when we all must give an account of our lives before him.

Boldly – not out of arrogance of our worth – but rather out of confidence in the work of Jesus on our behalf. Boldly approaching God because we have full assurance that Jesus has rendered us acceptable to him.

We can be bold because we are confident that Christ's death was sufficient to ransom many from death.

We can be bold because we are confident that Jesus offered the perfect sacrifice to secure for us complete forgiveness.

We can be bold because we know that Jesus is the High Priest, who always lives to intercede for us before God.

This confidence provides us with the certainty that all our stupid mistakes, all our most evil thoughts and actions, and every selfish act, can be forgiven, cleaned away by Jesus. Not only those in our past, but also every sin you will do in the future as well. None of it is beyond the value of Jesus' sacrifice to pay for, no sin is unforgiveable, none of it is beyond his will and ability to intercede for us and secure forgiveness for us before God.

> Our saviour has become the advocate of our weaknesses, so that we might be presented blameless before the throne of the father, for he stands at the right hand of the father, ever living to intercede for us.
>
> St. Athanasius of Alexandria (c. 296–373)
> *On the Incarnation*

Jesus invites even people like you and me to spiritually clean us. He welcomes us home to him, to a permanent peace with God. He wants to give us the absolute certainty that he loves us and will accept us forever.

No other relationship can give us that certainty that we are loved – and loved without conditions on how well we perform or behave. It is a love we cannot deserve but, therefore, *a love we cannot lose*. A love whose depth comes with the physical demonstration of Jesus giving his life for us on the cross.

This is the greatest news that any human can hear. God's permanent solution to our sin problem. Restoration of our relationship with him.

Why wouldn't you accept certain forgiveness from God and have a part in that?

In the next chapter we will consider how we can do just that.

CHAPTER NINE

Certain of a New Life

"I expect the resurrection of the dead, and the life of the age to come."
Nicene Creed

The Heartless Tyrant

Death begins its work in all of us from almost the beginning of our lives. Our bodies start to fail us and slowly deteriorate. Just like an old car, we have parts that need repairs, and others requiring replacements. The aches and pains spread. We do not recover from illness as rapidly as we did before. We slow down, we sleep more, and we do not think as sharply as we used to. Every time you catch a cold, or need an operation, or medications, this is the work of death in our bodies.

So, we spend billions of dollars a year to not only fix our broken bodies, but to prevent them failing in the first place. There are gym memberships, and exercise bikes, and magnets, and following the latest diet, and detox, and nutrition, and vitamin trends. We idolise and desire youth, so spend time and money attempting to appear younger. The Botox, hair replacement, surgery and cosmetics applied in an effort to convince others – and even fool ourselves – that we are still young. All in the hope that, by looking youthful, we can avoid the advance of death.

Even though we know that death is inevitable, we never find it acceptable. We value life, and strive to continue it. We are sad when someone takes their own life. Even in circumstances of a natural disaster, or an accident, or a serious and terminal illness, we commend people for 'fighting for life' or 'battling that disease'. We so value life that we consider the ultimate crime to be 'murder' and the ultimate penalty to be death. We know we have been made for life.

We mourn the death of those we love. The loss of my parents and brother continues to grieve me deeply. I feel their absence constantly, especially on their birthdays and at Easter and Christmas. I dream that it has all been a mistake, and we are reunited once more. But when I wake, I face the reality that death has taken them away. Nearly all of us will face that same grief. Those we love are taken away – the accidental deaths, those who die from disease, and those who die too young. It isn't right. Death fractures our relationships. Death parts us from those who love us and those whom we love.

When the death of the world's oldest person at 117 was recently mentioned in a late-night show monologue in a setup to a joke, the audience sighed with sadness rather than laughed. Death at any age is an offence to our deep conviction that we are made to live.

So hardwired is this conviction that children find the termination of life difficult to understand. Some parents try and shield their children from death, and others take great care when speaking of it. For the topic is confronting, and they ask questions we find difficult or impossible to answer. Just today our city's newspaper reported on a mother's challenge in the aftermath of the tragic death of her husband: "Just the other day, my four-year-old asked me: 'When is Daddy coming home from Heaven?' I had to explain to him that Daddy's not coming home. He was bawling his eyes out."[14] Death is incomprehensible. We are born assuming we were made for life, and that relationships are forever. Death is a cruel, heartless tyrant, which robs us of everything we value, and everyone we love.

We were made for Life

Our innate sense that we are made for life is confirmed by God in his word to us. In Genesis, the first book of the Bible, we can read that God created the first humans and placed them in the Garden of Eden. In the centre of the Garden was the Tree of Life, and therefore of human existence (Genesis 2:9). The writer of the book of Ecclesiastes describes how God made humanity with 'eternity in their hearts' – that deep within us we know that we are made for life. Even better, that we were made not simply for existence but so that we might 'rejoice and enjoy the good life' (Ecclesiastes 3:11-12).

However, through Adam and Eve sin entered the world. They rebelled against God's good commands by deciding they knew how to live better than God. Their penalty was exclusion from the Garden. The good world that God had made for us is spoiled by Sin. In Genesis chapter 3 the effects of sin are described – there is disharmony in relationships, pain where joy should be, frustration in work and, worst of all, death. Death is the direct result of sin (Romans 3:23). For outside of the Garden, they are cut off from the Tree of Life.

By nature, we were made for life. Death is unnatural and runs counter to our created purpose. It robs us of those things that give life value.

---

[14] "'He shouldn't be dead': Families sue Frankston Hospital over suicides" The Age, August 26, 2024

Death renders all things meaningless

As a doctor I have seen many people die and officially certified many deaths. Whether they were great or good, average or wicked, CEOs or Presidents or shopkeepers or accountants, husbands, wives, children, or uncles, who or what did they love, or who loved them- after death, I cannot tell any of these things about them. Bodily, they have come to nothing. Death robs us all, equally, of everything that matters.

What difference then does our life make if we all end at the same destination of nothingness? There is no meaning or purpose to anything we do. We are born without reason or purpose, and we struggle throughout our lives. Why be just and fair or loving when it comes to naught? There are no consequences, there is no justice. The good die the same as the evil. Why not be selfish and exploit others around us for our pleasure? If death terminates our existence, we may as well live to please ourselves in the time we have. Our achievements will be forgotten, or even criticised and dismantled, our wealth will be spent by others. For no matter who we are, or what we have achieved, who we have loved, or the money we have accumulated, they all end at death.

The great Russian author Leo Tolstoy expressed it this way:

> My question – that which at the age of fifty brought me to the verge of suicide – was the simplest of questions, lying in the soul of every man from the foolish child to the wisest elder: it was a question without an answer to which one cannot live, as I had found by experience. It was: 'What will come of what I am doing today or shall do tomorrow? What will come of my whole life?' Differently expressed, the question is: 'Why should I live, why wish for anything, or do anything?' It can also be expressed thus: 'Is there any

meaning in my life that the inevitable death awaiting me does not destroy?'[15]

But the cruellest of all is that we will be forgotten. The day will come when no one who knew and loved us will themselves be alive. No one will remember our favourite activities, or foods, or jokes, the way we smiled, or the joy we took in feeling the Sun on our face, or sharing a barbeque with family. Our lives will not have mattered. It will be as if we never existed. If death wins, our life amounts to nothing.

The Champion we Need

Yet we know there is one who has defeated death. We know because every year from Easter Sunday onwards Orthodox people greet each other with "Christ is Risen" and respond, "Truly he is risen". It is cemented into the foundations of Christian faith, because only victory over death can make life meaningful.

There is a story I have heard that is said to have occurred in the early days of Stalin's Soviet Union. I love this story even though it has all the hallmarks of an urban legend: it makes an attractive point, is probably impossible to verify and is magnified in the re-telling. However, even if untrue, its existence tells us something about the values held dear by those who spread it.

Nikolai Bukharin was a prominent member of Stalin's regime known for his aggressive propagation of atheism. The new Soviet Union was determined to purge the allegiances of any of its citizens to anything or anyone other than itself. Bukharin travelled from town to town delivering lectures

---

[15] *A Confession*, 1880 Leo Tolstoy

explaining that God did not exist, so that any faith in him was dangerously irrational and unpatriotic.

On one such occasion all of the citizens were forced to attend his lecture in their town hall. After two hours of monologue establishing the atheistic worldview, the triumphant conclusion was declared that God was dead and irrelevant. Bukharin's job in that town was completed. To his satisfaction, all faith in anyone or anything other than the state had been expunged.

In the silence after the lecture had concluded, a man mounted the stage and stood next to Bukharin. In a voice loud enough to be heard by all he declared "Christ is Risen". And all the audience, those presumed moments earlier to be atheistic devotees of the state, responded in unison, "Truly he has Risen".

The delight of the story is that it mocks a powerful man, who thought that by the strength of his position, and the appeal of his rhetoric, he could overturn the deeply ingrained beliefs of the people. But this episode demonstrated a far more significant point – that the people recognised that Godlessness is future-less. And, without a future, there is hopelessness. Everything comes to nothing. Even though the audience knew that in Stalin's Soviet Union people were 'disappeared' for causing much less offence to the regime than they gave that night, they knew it was worth it. For if there is no God then death wins.

Bukharin's argument was unacceptable because, without the hope of resurrection, life is unliveable. It was worth risking the retribution of the State to affirm that Christ had defeated death. For only if there is a future after death can life have meaning and purpose.

This is the truth that is so accurately and poetically expressed in the song sung in every Orthodox church early on Easter Sunday: Christ is risen, he has defeated death, he has rescued his people from the grave.

Christ is risen from the dead	Χριστός ανέστη εκ νεκρών
Trampling down death by death	θανάτω θάνατον πατήσας
and granting life to those in the tombs	και τοις εν τοις μνήμασι ζωήν χαρισόμενος

Every time you hear and sing each line of this song, it should excite in you the great victory Jesus won, and the promise of eternal life.

Christ is Risen

The empty tomb that the disciples discovered on that Sunday morning surprised them all. Yet Jesus had told them repeatedly that he would not only die, but also return to life.[16] They could not comprehend this when they first heard it, and only on later reflection did they remember that Jesus had done just as he promised.

> Jesus, having risen from the grave as he foretold, has granted us eternal life and great mercy.
>
> *Orthros of the Resurrection*

With only a missing body, the disciples remained unconvinced. However, over the next fifty days, their doubts were dispelled when they saw him many times. In fact, over 500 eyewitnesses saw the risen Jesus (1 Corinthians 15:6). He demonstrated that he was not merely a spirit, but that his body was physical by showing them the scars of his crucifixion, and by eating (John 20:27; Luke 24:36-43). In his physical body he returned to Heaven where he lives now and forever. In rising to life, Jesus had demonstrated that death was powerless to hold him. (If you are inter-

---

[16] Matt. 16:21, 17:22-23, 20:18-19, 27:63; Mark 8:31, 9:31, 10:33-34, 14:28; Luke 9:22, 18:31-33, 24:6-7; John 2:19-22.

ested in further evidence for the resurrection of Jesus, see 'A Word About the Resurrection' after the end of this chapter.)

Trampling down death by death

At the beginning of creation God had promised that one day he would send someone to reverse the curse of death. Humanity would not be left without hope. The serpent, Satan, had deceived Adam and Eve into sin and death. But to Satan, God declared,

> I will put hostility between you and the woman,
> and between your offspring and her offspring.
> He will strike your head,
> and you will strike his heel.
>
> Genesis 3:15

Jesus had been executed. He had faced the penalty for sin, and the angry judgement of God. Satan had done his utmost to conquer the Christ. But the Serpent had only nipped Jesus' heel.

However, in rising from the dead, Jesus accomplished an astonishing reversal. Through the very instrument of death that was intended to destroy him, Jesus turned the defeat upon Satan. Jesus crushed the head of Satan, disempowering him. Death itself was stamped underfoot.

In Australia we have frequent bushfires. These can destroy vast areas, the size of some small countries. Devastating heat of up to 1,100 degrees Celsius (about 2,000 F) clears all in its path, leaving behind blackened stumps and ashes. However, this destruction paves the way for new life. The fire clears out dead and decaying vegetation, releases nutrients into the soil, and makes space for sunlight to reach the bush floor. In time, the bush regrows, often healthier and more vibrant than before. The very process of death becomes the means by which renewal and new life are made possible for the bush.

By taking upon himself the sins of his people through death, Jesus took upon himself all the fires of judgement those sins deserved. So valuable was his life, so great his power, that all justice was served, all the power of death burnt itself out, all the anger of God at sin was extinguished on him. There was no more death left to die. All that was left was life. By his resurrection, Jesus demonstrated that he had freed, not only himself from death, but also liberated his people from its tyranny.

Granting Life to those in the Tombs

So, the apostle Paul can celebrate with the Corinthian Christians:

> When this corruptible body is clothed with incorruptibility, and this mortal body is clothed with immortality, then the saying that is written will take place:
>
> Death has been swallowed up in victory.
> Where, death, is your victory?
> Where, death, is your sting?
>
> The sting of death is sin, and the power of sin is the law. But thanks be to God, who gives us the victory through our Lord Jesus Christ!
>
> 1 Corinthians 15:54-57

I very clearly remember the first time, as a five-year-old, that a bee stung me on my foot. My small foot doubled in size and, burned in my memory, is the pain and the itch. Patients, young and old, continue to consult me, looking for relief from the agony of the sting – not to mention those who suffer allergic reactions.

What a relief it would be to us if no one had to fear a bee sting again. We could all happily walk barefoot through the grass without fear. Never again would a parent need to comfort their child in the aftermath of a sting.

In his victory over death, Jesus has removed the sting of death – the threat of death to destroy us, and to render all of life meaningless. No longer can death conquer Jesus' people, for they are liberated from its power. Instead, they can look forward to life.

For Jesus is not only resurrected to demonstrate his supremacy over death, but also to give new life to his people.

> But God, who is rich in mercy, because of his great love that he had for us, made us alive with Christ even though we were dead in trespasses. You are saved by grace! He also raised us up with him and seated us with him in the heavens in Christ Jesus, so that in the coming ages he might display the immeasurable riches of his grace through his kindness to us in Christ Jesus.
>
> Ephesians 2:4-7

It is sin that condemns us to death. But Christ brings life, and he takes his people with him. Even though they cannot experience Heaven now, their current location is in Heaven with Jesus. No longer dead in sin, they have a new life in Christ. Even better, they can look forward to that future day when they, too, can enjoy new unbreakable resurrection bodies, and they will fully experience God's gift of eternal life in his new creation.

Redeeming the Universe

For, if we only think of the plans of God as what he does for us, our thoughts are too small. For, through his resurrection Christ, does not just rescue *us* from death, he reverses the curse of sin upon the entire universe.

> For I consider that the sufferings of this present time are not worth comparing with the glory that is going to be revealed to us. For the creation eagerly waits with anticipation for God's sons to be revealed. For the creation was subjected to futility – not willingly, but because of him who subjected it – in the hope that the creation itself will also be set free from the bondage to decay into the glorious freedom of God's children. For we know that the whole creation has been groaning together with labour pains until now.
>
> Romans 8:18-22

As we saw in the beginning of this chapter, the rebellion of humanity corrupted the world. The good purposes for which God made it, became frustrated by our sin into those of disharmony, disaster, and death. But, through Jesus' resurrection, the effects of sin are reversed. New life comes, not only to us but to the whole universe, liberating us all.

In the passage from Romans above, the apostle Paul declares that this new future will be so glorious, that our current sufferings will be forgotten. In verse 22 he likens it to childbirth. Though the pain may be great, it is productive of great good. After childbirth is finished, I have often heard mothers announce that the pain was nothing in comparison to the joy of receiving the child in their arms.

So, says the apostle, will be our experience when we finally enter the new creation. The sufferings of this present time are real, but we will count them as nothing in comparison. They will be momentary, but Heaven will be forever. On the day someone wins the lottery, nobody remembers the parking fine. We will forget our present grief when, in the new creation, we embrace joy.

Later, in the book of Revelation, the apostle John describes this new creation as he is given a glimpse into Heaven:

> Then I saw a new Heaven and a new Earth; for the first Heaven and the first Earth had passed away, and the sea was no more. I also saw the holy city, the new Jerusalem, coming down out of Heaven from God, prepared like a bride adorned for her husband.
>
> |Then I heard a loud voice from the throne: Look, God's dwelling is with humanity, and he will live with them. They will be his peoples, and God himself will be with them and will be their God. He will wipe away every tear from their eyes. Death will be no more; grief, crying, and pain will be no more, because the previous things have passed away.
>
> Revelation 21:3-4

In this new creation there will be no more grief, crying or pain. Death will be abolished. God will establish a new creation where his good provision for us will never be challenged. It will be a beautiful new universe, where we can 'rejoice and enjoy the good life' that our hearts tell us is our goal, where God will live among us.

Leo Tolstoy came to realise that this promise from God can be trusted. He embraced the resurrection victory, which liberated him from death. He wrote: 'What meaning has life that death does not destroy? – Union with the eternal God: Heaven'.[17]

In Heaven, all of God's people will be gathered together by him. Yes, even the relationships fractured by death will be restored in God's new creation. We will, once again, be reunited with those in Christ whom we love. Imagine being together with those you thought were lost forever; imagine celebrating the greatness of Christ together with the ancestors you never met.

And we will have forever in which to enjoy this new creation, and one another, for God will grant us new resurrection bodies.

> You stretched out Your arms and united those who were divided of old. And, O Saviour, while restrained by the shroud and the tomb, You released those held in captivity who cry out:
> "There is none Holy, save You, O Lord."
>
> *Holy Saturday Liturgy*

A Resurrection Body

I loved playing competition football. Every year it was part of my winter routine and one of my great joys. That ended when my hip gave out. I am very thankful for a new hip, enabling me to walk, but I will never play again with this body. I wear glasses, my limbs are stiff, my blood pressure is high, and every day I take a handful of medication to stay alive. I will never again do a great many things with this body that I used to do. I am on the decline, and the inevitable path to death. We are all on that same path. This could be the cause of despair.

---

[17] *A Confession*, 1880 Leo Tolstoy

However, we have this promise:

> …we ourselves who have the Spirit as the firstfruits – we
> also groan within ourselves, eagerly waiting for adoption,
> the redemption of our bodies.
>
> Romans 8:23

Like creation, we too groan now, waiting for a new life to replace the frustration of the old. But, for those who follow Jesus, there is an exciting new future in which the struggles of this old life will be forgotten. No more fragile bodies, no more sickness, or pain, or anxiety, or grief, and no more death. No need to despair as our bodies fail us. For Jesus gives us new life. For each of us he has prepared a new resurrection body, incorruptible by sin or disease, unbreakable by death. A body in which we can fulfil our created purpose of glorifying God and enjoying him forever.

In December 2011, at the age of 50, one of my friends, Dave McDonald, found himself becoming increasingly short of breath. On a hectic day, he collapsed. Taken to the hospital, they discovered that his lungs had filled with fluid. After further tests, the doctors had bad news. A rare Stage IV Lung Cancer. He was given ten to 13 months to live.

In his book, *Hope Beyond Cure*, he describes how anyone receiving a diagnosis of terminal disease leaves them feeling confused, powerless, and grieving. A cure for them would be wonderful. Yet sickness returns for all of us, and one day we will all have to face death. So, Dave asks: 'where will we set our hope when the inevitable day arrives, and death knocks on the door?'[18] He answers by pointing to a more enduring hope available to us all.

> This hope of eternity is not wishful thinking for pie in the
> sky when we die. It's real and anchored in history. It comes

---

[18] *Hope Beyond Cure*, 2013 p68

from Jesus Christ and his victory over death. Let's put our hope in Jesus Christ. Let's turn to him, depend on him and take hold of everything he offers. We don't have to love without hope. There's a real hope, an eternal hope, and it can be ours. God wants us to know this hope, to take hold of it ourselves.

It's worth investigating the promises of God: if they're true, then we have absolutely nothing to lose and absolutely everything to gain.

Hope Beyond Cure, p 69

Some of us might arrive there quicker than others, but we will all eventually need the same thing. A new body. Jesus' resurrection guarantees his people just that.

This life will one day come to an end for me, but a new one awaits. I like to think of it as if I'm looking forward to a much-anticipated trip. The tickets have been purchased, my bags are packed, and my passport is stamped. All of this has been arranged by Jesus, and not me, so I can be sure that I will be going. Now I only need wait and look forward to the never-ending adventure of a new lifetime. I can't wait!

Will you join us?

By Your resurrection, You transformed Your corruptible body to incorruption and made it a source of life incorruptible.

Holy Saturday Liturgy

No one need fear death; the Saviour's death has freed us from it...
You brought us out of nothing into being, and when we had fallen away, You raised us up again. You left ***nothing undone*** until you had led us up to Heaven and granted us Your kingdom, which is to come.

Orthros of the Resurrection

Blessed be the God and Father of our Lord Jesus Christ. Because of his great mercy he has given us new birth into a living hope through the resurrection of Jesus Christ from the dead and into an inheritance that is imperishable, undefiled, and unfading, kept in heaven for you.

1 Peter 1:3-4

A WORD ABOUT THE RESURRECTION

The resurrection of Jesus has been disputed since its very occurrence. However, the evidence is so overwhelming, and convincing, that the Christian Church remains unshaken in its conviction that Jesus rose from the dead.

Many lawyers have considered the evidence for the resurrection from a legal perspective and concluded that, beyond reasonable doubt, Jesus did rise from the dead. One of them was a British lawyer, Sir Norman Anderson, wrote about it in his short booklet, *The Evidence for the Resurrection*.

Even sceptics who have examined the evidence have become convinced. An example is Frank Morrison who was motivated to study the story of Christ because he felt it rested on fragile foundations. He resolved to write a book examining the final days of Jesus, stripped of what, he thought, were primitive beliefs of the supernatural reinforced by Church dogma. However, the book he eventually wrote, *Who Moved the Stone?*, had as its first chapter 'The Book that Refused to be Written'. For the further he delved into the evidence, and the more questions he asked, the firmer he became convinced – the only possible conclusion is that the resurrection of Jesus was a historical reality.

Another interesting book is *The Resurrection of Jesus: A Jewish Perspective* by Pinchas Lapide. Rabbi Lapide was not a follower of Jesus, yet he found the evidence establishing that Jesus had risen from the dead to be indisputable.

There are many other books (and no doubt websites) that present the evidence in as much detail as you require.

Briefly, from my perspective, here are some of the points of evidence to consider:

1. Jesus was definitely dead. The spear that was driven into Jesus released 'blood and water'. It means they hit either his heart, or a major vessel, plus the fluid that accumulates around the lungs and heart with cardiac failure. If Roman soldiers knew anything, it was how to kill someone.

2. Roman soldiers guarded Jesus' tomb, and all soldiers knew the penalty for failing their duty was death (compare Acts 12:19).

3. The Jewish and Roman authorities, who opposed Christianity, could have stamped it out from the beginning simply by presenting the body – but Jesus was not in the tomb.

4. Instead, Christianity grew rapidly, which would not have occurred if questions about Jesus' resurrection remained.

5. The disciples were radically transformed, from those who fled the crucifixion to those (all but one) who would suffer and die for preaching about a resurrected saviour (Mark 14:50; Acts 5:29-33).

6. More than 500 eyewitnesses testified to seeing the risen Jesus (1 Corinthians 15:6).

7. Most were still alive when the New Testament was written and could have been questioned and challenged. This was not an event in the distant past, relying on hazy memories. The earliest writings were only 20 years after the event. It would be like writing about 9-11 today and being able to verify what had happened from all the eyewitness accounts. Were someone to claim that a momentous event, like the Resurrection, or 9-11, had happened when it could easily be disproven by those who were there, they would lose all credibility, and Christianity would have proceeded no further.

8. Jesus said he would die and be raised again, and he did everything else he promised to do, including bringing others back from death.

9. Old Testament prophecies promised the Messiah's resurrection (e.g. Psalm 16:8-10, Isaiah 53:10-12) and that he would rule his people forever (eg Isaiah 9:6-7, Daniel 2:44,7:14).

10. Accounts of the resurrection include inconvenient truths that one would not have included in a fabricated story, like the fact that women were the first witnesses. In the first century, a woman's testimony was not considered valid evidence (Matthew 28:1-10, John 20:11-18).

A WORD ABOUT JUSTICE AND JUDGEMENT

I love organised crime movies. Goodfellas, Casino, Scarface, The Untouchables. The original, and probably the best, was The Godfather, with Marlon Brando portraying the patriarch of the Corleone crime family. I think the appeal to me is seeing what someone does with unfettered power.

Corleone's crime syndicate ruthlessly exerts control through beatings, assassinations, bribes and intimidation. They operate outside of the law and become victors in a gangland war, appearing to act without consequences. The end of Vito Corleone's life was in his backyard amongst his tomato vines. There he was enjoying his twilight years. As he played with his grandson, he finally succumbs to death. He dies the respectable grandfather, full of years and in peace. There is no violent end for him, no body dumped in an unmarked grave, no being hounded into poverty like those who crossed his path. An evil man dying in peace after profiting from destroying the lives of others.

While The Godfather was only a movie, it portrayed a pattern we see played out all too often in the real world. The wealthy and powerful harm and exploit the poor and weak. While their victims suffer, they live prosperous lives, never having to answer for their crimes. We see it in the innocent victims of war, those who get killed while fleeing and those who remain, who are robbed, raped, and murdered. There are so many that they cannot be remembered, and the incidents are so shrouded by the fog of war that their culprits never face justice.

We see it in the hidden crimes committed against those who cannot, or dare not, report it. Just this week there was another story of the hundreds of assaults perpetrated by a multi-millionaire that have only come to light after his death. So powerful was this man that even the media, who knew of his crimes, were afraid to report them. Add to them the exploitation of the powerless. The illegal immigrants enticed to another country, who work for next to nothing in fear of being reported to the authorities. The shameful abuses that are committed against the defenceless that happen behind closed doors. The neglect of the vulnerable who deserve our care – the children, the aged, the disabled. The victims who are so weak in the eyes of society, or are too young, or do not know how to obtain justice, or don't trust the police, or simply aren't fluent enough to speak. If they do make a report they may be ignored, or their case mishandled. Justice is biased towards the articulate and wealthy.

Then there are the injustices that we all face personally – some great, some small. My family was decimated in the second world war by the neglect and abuse of an occupying force, but none were held to account for their deaths. They fled Europe for a better life in Australia, to face different brands of racist abuse, robbery, and exploitation.

You will have your own stories that have affected you personally, and the ones you love. They can be harrowing, crushing, and fill you with despair with trauma, ongoing across generations. You might still experience daily grief from your mistreatment at the hands of others. It leaves us to wonder if there can be justice. Will those, who have so burdened others by their evil behaviour, ever have to answer for what they have done?

Justice in a godless world

If there is no God, then the answer to this question is quite straightforward. According to the self-described atheist commentator, Richard Dawkins:

> Nature is not cruel, only pitilessly indifferent. This is one of
> the hardest lessons for humans to learn. We cannot admit

that things might be neither good nor evil, neither cruel nor kind, but simply callous – indifferent to all suffering, lacking all purpose.[19]

In a godless world, our desire for justice is an aberration. There is no right, there is no wrong, there is only randomness. Cockroaches get trodden on, cars kill wildlife, people are murdered – it's all the same. Stuff happens, that's all. Everything is meaningless. Your feelings of hurt, as well as your compassion for those who are suffering, are all misguided and inappropriate. You cannot complain and, even if you tried, there is no-one to whom you can complain. There is no justice. Power over others is all that matters, for then you can act as you please without consequence. Might makes right.

The problem with this answer is that it is an entirely unsatisfying, unliveable philosophy of life. We know people matter. Their lives are significant, and valuable. It is not a nothing to rob someone of their dignity, integrity, goods, or life to take them for yourself. The notion of justice is so hardwired into us that one of the most common complaints children make about others' behaviour is that 'it's not fair'. Caring about what happens to people, and wanting to protect them, is what justice is all about.

In this, Richard Dawkins is correct. In an impersonal, godless universe, everything is random, no one cares, and the very concept of justice is meaningless.

However, there is a God, and he is committed to seeing justice done.

---

[19] *River Out of Eden: A Darwinian View of Life* (1995), 112

God is Committed to Justice

Jesus told a story to encourage people to bring their requests for justice to God.

> There was a judge in a certain town who didn't fear God or respect people. And a widow in that town kept coming to him, saying, 'Give me justice against my adversary'.
>
> Luke 18:1-3

A woman approaches a judge in search of justice. We are not told what the issue was – it could have been theft, perhaps a land dispute, maybe something has been stolen from her, like the livestock she depends upon for her livelihood, or maybe she had been assaulted, leaving her feeling vulnerable.

But whatever the injustice against her, she is a widow. Without a husband in that society, she would struggle to make an income and be considered defenceless. So, she turns to the one who should be concerned for justice, and that is the unnamed judge.

An unjust judge

Even the best of our present-day justice systems are imperfect. They are slow, under-resourced, and sometimes cannot obtain or consider all the evidence, or can make mistakes. But at least, for the most part, they are people trying their best.

However, this widow's judge in verse 2 'didn't fear God or respect people'. This judge is not concerned for his reputation within society. He does not acknowledge his accountability to human authorities, not even to God. Subsequently he is a judge who is unmotivated to provide justice, but only works to further his own power, influence and comfort. All of this means that this widow's only hope in securing justice is a very poor one.

Yet without anyone else to whom to turn this woman keeps on pestering the unjust judge. The widow kept coming to him: "give me justice, give me justice, give me justice." This was a determined woman. Day after day the same demand: "give me justice!"

The Judge gives in

Eventually, her persistence pays off because the result is that *even this judge* gives in.

> For a while he was unwilling, but later he said to himself, 'Even though I don't fear God or respect people, yet because this widow keeps pestering me, I will give her justice, so that she doesn't wear me out by her persistent coming.'
>
> Luke 18:4-5

There is a wonderfully evocative phrase here. Where we read 'wear me out' a more literal translation is 'I will give her justice, so that she does not **give me a black eye** by her persistent coming'. The repeated verbal haranguing from this woman is like a physical assault on this judge. So, even though he only cares about himself, he gives her the justice she seeks.

God stands in contrast to this judge

The point of Jesus' story is not to describe how God is *like* this judge. That is, it's not about the immense power of nagging God – that by repeatedly asking God he will eventually give in. Jesus says, in his instructions about the Lord's prayer, that we are not to be like the pagans who think they are heard because of their many words. God is not a God who needs to be nagged for attention. Nor is it that God needs to be bullied to comply with our demands because he is lazy and unjust.

Instead, the point of the parable is to show how God is **unlike** the unjust judge. It is not a comparison of God with the judge, but a *contrast*.

> Then the Lord said, "Listen to what the unjust judge says. Will not God grant justice to his elect who cry out to him day and night? Will he delay helping them? I tell you that he will swiftly grant them justice."
>
> Luke 18:6-8

Jesus calls attention to the judge's words to highlight the difference. This judge must be pestered because he has no concern for anyone but himself. But, in contrast, God is not reluctant but is *eager* to provide justice for his people. The point of Jesus' story is that if this dishonest judge yields to the cry from a helpless, lowly widow, then **how much more** will the loving God grant his people the justice they desire. Bring your requests for justice to God and he will deliver it without delay.

God Delivers Complete Justice

However, what does God mean when he speaks of 'justice'? How does he promise to deliver it?

The clever people who think about these things identify four basic categories of justice. Seeing as we in the West have had our notions of justice shaped by the Bible, it is unsurprising that all four are those with which God addresses.

Procedural justice – that everyone will be treated fairly and impartially and receive what is right. We have already seen that God is powerful, good and loving. He cannot be swayed by bribes or favouritism and will deliver a just verdict.

Restorative justice – which is restoring to affected people that which the injustice took from them. This is straightforward when their car is stolen, but more difficult when it is their dignity, or sense of security.

Yet, as we saw in Chapter Nine, that is exactly what God does for us in the new creation. There will be no more suffering or evil. No longer will anyone be exploited or harmed. All will be treated fairly. For those in this new creation will be transformed to be like Jesus. So that no longer will we be selfish, and mistreat one another, for there will no longer be sin.

We will also have new resurrection bodies that will no longer grieve, or cry, or be anxious. The damage done to us by others will be wiped away. So glorious will be our new life that we will not remember the pain of the past. It will be a new existence in a new world. All things will be restored, as if sin and evil had never entered the world or our lives.

This is also where God will deliver **distributive justice** – everyone receiving their fair share. For there will no longer be the rich and poor, the strong and the weak, the powerful and the vulnerable. All will be richly blessed by God, and none will be in need.

But God does not forget the evil done previously. Before he establishes his new creation, he will ensure that all past wrongdoing receives the punishment it deserves. This is called **retributive justice**. God is committed to punishing injustice because he loves us.

The Loving Judge

> Lord, God of vengeance –
> God of vengeance, shine!
> Rise up, Judge of the earth;
> repay the proud what they deserve.
> Lord, how long will the wicked –
> how long will the wicked celebrate?
> They pour out arrogant words;
> all the evildoers boast.
> Lord, they crush your people;
> they oppress your heritage.
> They kill the widow and the resident alien
> and murder the fatherless.
>
> Psalm 94:1-6

As we have already observed, the 'natural', sinful way to think of human worth is to make it about power. The mighty are valuable, for they can offer others favours, and have money, influence, and physical might to accomplish their goals. The powerless cannot help others or defend themselves. They have no value. So, in the verses of this Psalm, the crime of the strong is to crush and kill the defenceless widows, aliens (immigrants), and fatherless. Their lives are considered cheap to the mighty. They have no claim to justice, for they are of no value. And once life is worthless, then everything is permissible, and there is no limit to the evil that can be done.

Our God's standards, however, stand in stark contrast. God created all people, male and female, in his image. All are therefore of equal value. God plays no favourites. God wants no one to be denied the blessings of life that he provides.

So, when these evildoers treat the vulnerable as of lesser value than themselves, they call God into question. God takes seriously the dignity of all people so, when they are harmed, God is outraged with fury. God does not turn away when innocent people suffer, nor is he indifferent to their pain, for that would be unloving. He cares deeply about all people and will not excuse their tormentors or let them escape without consequences. God will bring retribution against these evildoers out of love for those wronged.

But the perpetrators are arrogant. They think they can act without consequences.

Nothing escapes God's notice

> They say, "The Lord doesn't see it.
> The God of Jacob doesn't pay attention."
> Pay attention, you stupid people!
> Fools, when will you be wise?
> Can the one who shaped the ear not hear,
> the one who formed the eye not see?
> The one who instructs nations,
> the one who teaches mankind knowledge –
> does he not discipline?
>
> Psalm 94:7-10

These evildoers live as if they will not be accountable to God, thinking that their deeds have been unnoticed. But, unlike human judges, God does not need to be alerted to wrongdoing for nothing escapes him.

God sees what people do when they think they are hidden. God looks inside us all, and sees our thoughts and motivations. The evil that is done that no person ever sees, where no evidence is left, that will never come before a court – God sees it all. The offence which people ignore, or where the perpetrator is protected, or where money, or power, buy them out of trouble – God remembers. When people plot against you, when prejudice denies people of opportunity, when others are undermined by gossip and slander, and no one knows the culprits, and the victims are not believed – God knows and believes. He even sees when those in our courts, and police, and all those in government, and in positions of power over us, act unjustly. God sees and knows all, and will hold them responsible for their wrongdoing.

So, when God sees injustice like this:

> They band together against the life of the righteous
> and condemn the innocent to death.
>
> Psalm 94:21

this is his response:

> He will pay them back for their sins
> and destroy them for their evil.
> The Lord our God will destroy them.
>
> Psalm 94:23

Whatever injustices you have endured, or continue to suffer from in your life, God will personally see that justice is done. The guilty will not be acquitted, and God will bring destruction upon them. 'Vengeance belongs to me; I will repay, says the Lord' (Romans 12:19). Those who have wronged you will be repaid in full by God.

The comfort this provides is knowing that we do not have to pursue our earthly tormentors in fear that they will avoid consequences for their crimes. We can trust that our all-seeing, always just, God will hold them accountable. We can rest, knowing that God's punishment will fit the crime, and that there is nothing we can do to improve on his justice. For his punishment is terrible and complete. As we saw in chapter 3, the just penalty for sin to be excluded from God's presence in the eternal destruction of Hell.

The Day of Judgement

This will happen at the end of time when God finalises his judgement.

> I also saw the dead, the great and the small, standing before the throne, and books were opened. Another book was opened, which is the book of life, and the dead were judged according to their works by what was written in the books.
>
> Revelation 21:12

Once again we hear from the apostle John as he is given a vision inside Heaven at the end of time. There he witnesses the day of judgement, where books are opened listing all of our works – another way of telling us that God has missed nothing. Then all will be judged according to what they have done. None will escape judgement, and justice will be done. And on the basis of our works, we will all be found guilty.

Except for those whose judgement has already been completed.

For God started his final judgement at the cross. It is there that we can know that God will keep his word, to repay evil on that final day.

Final Judgement started at the Cross

In the death of Christ, God pours out his judgement upon him. That is why the sky darkens and the Earth quakes. It is why Jesus exclaims, "My God, my God, why have you abandoned me?"[20] For Jesus is experiencing God turning his back on him. Jesus is taking the penalty of death that our sin deserves, in the place of his people.

Here we see God's commitment to justice. Though he loves his people, God does not play favourites. He does not overlook their sin. To be unwaveringly just, he must punish sin, even when it comes at the great cost of the life of his son.

> For we were enemies of God through sin, and God had appointed the sinner to die. There must needs therefore have happened one of two things; either that God, in his truth, should destroy all men, or that in his loving-kindness he should cancel the sentence. But behold the wisdom of God; he preserved both the truth of his sentence, and the exercise of his loving-kindness. Christ took our sins in his body on the tree, that we by his death might die to sin, and live unto righteousness.
>
> St. Cyril of Jerusalem

When we look at the cross, we can have confidence that God is an impartial judge. We can believe his promise that all will receive what they deserve on that final day. Each and every wrong will be repaid with flawless justice. God doesn't overlook a single crime or lighten a single sentence. He will either nail the sin to the cross, or he will punish it eternally in Hell. We will see justice done. God will avenge every offence against us.

---

[20] Matthew 27:46

Justice delayed

But for now, we wait.

> Above all, be aware of this: Scoffers will come in the last
> days scoffing and following their own evil desires, saying,
> "Where is his 'coming' that he promised? Ever since our
> ancestors fell asleep, all things continue as they have been
> since the beginning of creation."
> Dear friends, don't overlook this one fact: With the Lord
> one day is like a thousand years, and a thousand years like
> one day. The Lord does not delay his promise, as some
> understand delay, but is patient with you, not wanting any
> to perish but all to come to repentance.
>
> 2 Peter 3:3-4, 8-9

When we see injustice around us, or when we experience it ourselves,
we simply want it to end. God sees all injustices, he knows our pain, and he
desires, more than us, to end evil in this world. God has set a Day when he
will redress all wrongs and wipe the world clean. So that pain and suffering
never return, he will also remove all who have perpetrated evil. The problem is that this includes all of us.

So God delays his judgement, to give all people an opportunity to turn
back to him. He wants them to avoid his terrible anger by following Jesus,
by accepting his offer to stand in their place. These are those who are written in the Book of Life, who escape God's judgement, who are welcome
into Heaven.

God waits to restore justice for what seems to us a long time. But God's
timing is not ours. God 'is gracious and compassionate, slow to anger and

great in faithful love'.[21] God waits to give people time to escape the coming judgement, which he warns us we will all have to face.

In the 1990s in the US there was an ad campaign with the slogan 'Friends Don't Let Friends Drive Drunk'. It encouraged people to make that uncomfortable suggestion to their friends that they were too intoxicated to drive. The result was a dramatic fall in alcohol-related vehicle fatalities, for people loved their friends enough to warn them away from heading for disaster.

God loves us. He loves us more deeply than we can ever imagine.

But understand this:

God is *NOT* on your side.

God is on the side of justice.

God will avenge the harm done to all his beloved creatures. But not just the wrongs done *to* us – but also the wrongs done *by* us. And God has promised to bring destruction on all who stand unforgiven before him on that judgement day.

But again, out of his love, God warns us of the certainty of this disaster. He urges us to stop living for ourselves, and to turn to serve Jesus. For an even greater demonstration of God's love is his provision of the only way to escape that judgement. He generously gave his son to stand in the place of judgement for us, to secure our complete forgiveness – if only we will accept it.

It is right for us to yearn for justice for our world. It is right for us to long for relief from what we continue to suffer from the wrongs committed against us. We can take comfort that God is aware of our pain, and he sees and will repay all the evil ever committed. He has promised to establish justice, and to restore us permanently. But ensure you are on the right side

---

[21] Psalm 145:8-9

of judgement on that day. Make sure that you are at peace with God by following Jesus. Only then can you be certain of forgiveness and eternal life. But more about that certainty in the next chapter.

CHAPTER TEN

Certain Peace with God

During each of my high school years, all the students were transported to a nearby park to run a cross-country course. It was compulsory to compete. Four or five kilometres along dirt paths, up and down hillocks, and dodging tree branches.

I would start out strong, trying to keep up with the front-runners. But every year it was apparent I had gone out too hard. I lacked the stamina to keep up with them and fell behind. Some years I didn't finish at all.

We can think of our life journey with God like that race. We want to put in our best effort, yet we know we cannot be consistent the whole way. Sometimes we run faster, other times we fall down, or go completely off track. We know we cannot be sure that we have the stamina to finish the race running it for God.

And we are correct to doubt ourselves. As we have seen, we continue to sin throughout our lives, to fall short of God's standards, to disappoint him. We find ourselves distracted away from living for God. We are right to conclude we will never be good enough for God. So, can we have any confidence that we can live our life, and finish it as one of God's people?

The apostle Paul answers this question in his letter to the Roman Christians. In his answer, he does not concern himself with our performance – our goodness, or how we have run our race, or how strong has been our belief in God. These are irrelevant to the question. Instead, Paul declares that our salvation depends entirely *on God* and not at all on us. In this passage he excitedly piles reason upon reason to give us confidence that, no matter what, God will securely keep us until, and beyond, the end.

God always carries out his plans

> We know that all things work together for the good of those who love God, who are called according to his purpose. For those he foreknew he also predestined to be conformed to the image of his Son, so that he would be the firstborn among many brothers and sisters. And those he predestined, he also called; and those he called, he also justified; and those he justified, he also glorified.
>
> Romans 8:28-30

From before creation, God chose a people to bless. Through his plan he justified them, meaning that he declared them right, counting them innocent of sin. Ultimately, he glorified them by transforming them to become like Jesus.

See what superb honour! For what the Only-begotten was by Nature, this they also have become by grace.

John Chrysostom, *Homilies*

Notice that Paul is not speaking of the future, but of the present. God has already done this for his people. There is no requirement for them to make progress, or maintain a certain level of obedience, to merit peace with God. Instead, God has transformed them to become holy and acceptable – right now.

God has done all this because he planned it before the beginning of time. God is entirely trustworthy, he always keeps his promises, always keeps his commitments. His purposes will always be completed. God is so in control that, as verse 28 says, everything in the lives of God's people will work towards their ultimate good – that of being brought safely into eternal life.

So, in verse 31 Paul can conclude,

> What, then, are we to say about these things? If God is for us, who is against us?
>
> Romans 8:31

God cannot be outmanoeuvred, nor can he be overpowered – he is God. So, if God is on our side, then it does not matter what or who stands against us – nobody can defeat us. To which we might say – of course that is true, but that is a big 'if'. How can we know that God is on our side?

God gave us His Son

> He did not even spare his own Son but gave him up for us all. How will he not also with him grant us everything?
>
> Romans 8:31-32

The price that God paid to rescue us from sin and death was unimaginable. He gave up the son with whom he had been united in love for all eternity.

Yet he loved us so much that, even though we were his enemies, he sent Christ to die for us. He gave us Jesus to stand in the place of judgement that we deserved.

If God gave us his most precious son, God become man, the most valuable of all beings, how can we question if he is on our side? How can we doubt that he will give us everything we need, namely salvation and eternal life?

In the occupied Athens of 1941, food was scarce. Every morning it was not uncommon for my father to walk in the street past the bodies of those who had starved to death overnight. His mother would travel great distances to find her children food, further and further each day as food supplies dwindled. She would return to their home and prepare the food for the family but seldom ate herself. Malnutrition took her before the occupation's end. She gave her very life so that her children could live – so that my father would live and, in turn, so I could live. Who could question her love for her children when she had made the supreme sacrifice? Having given her life, no-one could doubt that she would give anything to her beloved family.

God has given us his most precious Jesus. We cannot doubt his love and generosity towards us. Having given us Jesus makes us sure he will withhold none of his blessings from us.

> See, what great things he hath given unto us! Doubt not then about the future.
>
> John Chrysostom, *Homilies*

This would be evidence enough. Yet there is more.

No guilt remains

One of the titles given in the Bible to Satan is that of accuser. He is described as constantly bringing charges before God against his people:[22] 'they are faithless, sinners, selfish, consider the evil they do, look at how often they fail You, they only serve You because you bless them.'[23] They are, in fact, the kinds of accusations we bring against ourselves. Surely, accuses Satan, all people are guilty, and none deserve forgiveness.

But God has an answer to Satan, and to everyone who believes God should condemn us.

> Who can bring an accusation against God's elect? God is the one who justifies. Who is the one who condemns? Christ Jesus is the one who died, but even more, has been raised; he also is at the right hand of God and intercedes for us.
>
> Romans 8:33-34

God sees our lives, hears our thoughts, and knows our hearts. Our failures come as no surprise to him – he has told us himself that we will continue to sin[24]. Additionally, God is a just judge. He cannot overlook evil, and will always apply the punishment it deserves. God knows the charges against us are accurate and agrees that, yes, just as Satan asserts, we merit condemnation.

However, when in the court of God's judgement charges are brought against us, we have a defence lawyer to plead our case. It is Jesus who is more than our advocate, for he steps forward and offers to stand in our

---

[22] Revelation 12:10; Zechariah 3:3
[23] Job 1:8-10; Job 2:3-5
[24] 1 John 1:8

place and accept the punishment for our sin. He intercedes for us forever, exchanging our guilt for his innocence.

That is why Paul can declare that no accusation will be effective. God has already accepted Jesus' death as payment in full for the guilt of his people. As a result, God has justified his people, declared him eternally innocent before him. No matter who accuses them or of what crime, all guilt has been expunged, all penalty has been paid, there is no more sin left for which they must give account. Whoever accepts the death of Jesus is right with God from now and into eternity.

God will Always Love Us

That is why Paul continues,

> Who can separate us from the love of Christ? Can affliction or distress or persecution or famine or nakedness or danger or sword? As it is written:
>
> Because of you
> we are being put to death all day long;
> we are counted as sheep to be slaughtered.

Romans 8:35-36

The Apostle warns us that this life will not be care-free. There will be the suffering and hard times, and the struggles and death that are both common to all people, as well as those particularly aimed at Christians. This is all part of living in a world that has been corrupted by our sin, by our evil. God is not promising that his people will escape those challenges. It's at those times we might find ourselves wondering if God has deserted us.

Instead, we are being reminded that, no matter what life throws up, God will not abandon us. Even when things are at their worst, the love of Christ is guaranteed.

More than conquerors

> No, in all these things we are more than conquerors through
> him who loved us.
>
> Romans 8:37

I love the Greek word here translated 'more than conquerors': *hypernikomen* (ὑπερνικῶμεν). It means 'super-victorious' or 'hyper-winners'. It's saying that God's people are the most victorious of all the winners. For God will always love them and has granted them salvation. So complete and overwhelming is their triumph, that eternal life is guaranteed. How exciting is that!

Labelling Christians as more than conquerors stands in stark contrast to their appearance in the world. Elsewhere Paul calls Christians the refuse (rubbish) of the world, because they are persecuted for following Jesus. Christians are not impressive in the world's terms because they embrace humility not power; they trust in God and not in their personal strength. Their triumph does not come from being super powerful or incredibly wealthy. It is not a reward for their greatness. It is the gift of God.

And this victory transforms these powerless ones into those who are granted a victory greater than any that could be achieved by an Emperor or President or Billionaire. For even their great earthly power cannot acquire salvation and life eternal, for no person can merit that. Only God can do it.

And because it depends on God, this victory is guaranteed. God's people can be completely assured they will be more than conquerors in every circumstance and at every time.

> For I am persuaded that neither death nor life, nor angels nor rulers, nor things present nor things to come, nor powers, nor height nor depth, nor any other created thing will be able to separate us from the love of God that is in Christ Jesus our Lord.
>
> Romans 8:38-39

Nothing can separate God's people from his love. In all of life, God is there for his people. They are already justified, already saved, already transformed into the likeness of Jesus. In death there is no more that God's people must do to become acceptable, for God is still there loving them. There are no powers, either natural or supernatural, that can stop God. There are no places in the universe where God cannot find us. There are no current or future circumstances that will somehow surprise God. God is in control of all powers, all things, and all time, and he has committed to loving his people.

When loving parents are expecting the birth of their first child, even before they meet them, they decide that they will love them. After they are born, such parents continue to protect and love them for the rest of their lives. No matter what they do, their parents are there for them.

If human parents, sinful as we all are, can commit to a love like that, how much more does God? He is the God who can do all that he plans to do. He is the God who cannot lie and always keeps his promises. He is the God whose very character is love. God will never abandon us.

Recall in Chapter Two where I asked you the question: 'If you were to die tonight and come before God, would he let you into his Heaven?' What was your answer? If it was 'no' or 'not sure' you now have an opportunity to change that to '*yes*'. You can be completely certain that God will welcome you, because it depends only on God holding onto *us*, not us holding onto him. We will stumble, and we will disappoint ourselves and God, for we are sinful. But it is God who will make us endure, trusting and serving him until the end. God's people are right with him now and will remain his forever. We can be assured that God's salvation is ours both now and forever.

There is a glorious future awaiting us all – if we join God and accept what he has done for us in Christ. Let's find out how we can follow Jesus in part 3.

> And this is the testimony: God has given us eternal life, and this life is in his Son. The one who has the Son has life. The one who does not have the Son of God does not have life. I have written these things to you who believe in the name of the Son of God so **that you may know that you have eternal life.**
>
> 1 John 5:11-13

ZACHARY'S STORY

My name is Zachary, I am 62 years of age, formerly an accountant and now a minister of religion, husband of a beautiful wife, father of three gorgeous daughters, and grandfather of nine fabulous grandchildren.

I was raised in a Greek family with a casual, yet warm, awareness of Jesus Christ, which focussed on religious observance (Easter, religious festivals, infant baptism) in the hope of being in the good books with a distant and vague God.

Dedicated and loving women, from a Bible-believing church, taught me the Bible when I was five years of age. I was sent to a local Sunday School because the nearest Greek Orthodox church was quite a distance away from our family home, and a woman, who believed in the Bible, befriended my mother and encouraged her that attending the Sunday School would be good for me. My mother was open to this, partly because although she was Greek, she was born and raised in France, and therefore she was exposed to other religious teachings. Further, when she came to Australia, she had a series of people wishing to read the Bible with her. My mother was therefore not tied to any particular church tradition and, indeed, was used by the Lord to give me an awareness of spiritual realities and prayer.

I immediately accepted the message that was taught to me by those who understood the importance of teaching the scriptures to elicit faith in the hearers. This is when I realised that God was the ruler of the world and, if I wanted to be in good standing with him, I needed to obey him and have Jesus in my life.

In the years that followed my initial encounter with Bible teaching, I would be taken by my parents to various Greek religious church services and activities, while continuing to be taught the Bible by non-Greeks most other Sundays. This meant that the extended family networks of uncles, aunts and cousins thought I was a bit strange, but they never shunned me, and we continue to have warm connections to this day.

During my teenage years I had no certainty of salvation, and I was terrified of dying in my sleep, not knowing if I would be saved and welcomed into Heaven. This was perhaps because of the influence in my life of some religious people who, contrary to what the Bible teaches, would assert I needed to contribute to my salvation in order to be saved, and I was never sure I had done enough, or asked God for forgiveness of every possible sin I may have unknowingly committed. When I raised my insecurity about my eternal future with someone, once again it was a believer in the Bible who influenced me, and showed me that in the Bible why I can be absolutely certain of going to Heaven, because of what Jesus has already done for me. This, they asserted, cannot be erased nor extinguished, despite my shortcomings and failures.

During my early twenties, my father received a 4:30am telephone call from the father of a Greek friend of mine (who was studying medicine and reading the Bible with me). He told my father that if I ever contacted his son again, he would kill me. This demonstrated to me how evil some people can be, going to extreme measures to deny someone else exposure to the words of eternal life, as found in the Bible. This merely strengthened my resolve to devote my life to the sharing of the message of the Bible to others.

So, I seek to live a life of obedience to my Lord, because I have found certain salvation in Jesus as he has revealed himself to me through his word, the Bible, and not in an ecclesiastical institution or ritual which cannot offer certainty.

During the times I was uncertain of my salvation, this message gave me real and definite comfort, and remains close to my heart today:

John 3:36 says: *Whoever believes in the Son has eternal life, but whoever rejects the Son will not see life, for God's wrath remains on him.*

PART 3

How Must I Respond?

CHAPTER ELEVEN

Turn Back

Offensive Jesus

The people of ancient Israel occupied a uniquely privileged place in history. They were the people chosen by God. They were marked as his special people by circumcision, food laws and festivals. The symbolic earthly throne of God in the Temple was in their midst, and through their priests, they could approach God with sacrifices and prayers. They operated on God-given laws of justice that we continue to value and observe to this day. Additionally, God had promised a future day when their special anointed King would arrive to liberate them.

In the 1ˢᵗ century AD, the glory days of Israel were long past, and what remained of the nation was under Roman occupation. So, they looked forward all the more to this Messiah who would take their side, affirm their special status with God, and declare judgement on the Gentile (non-Jewish) world.

On the arrival of Jesus, many believed him to be the long-promised King sent by God. Finally, they hoped, their salvation was here. They longed for him to fix their world. Jesus drew crowds, anticipating their Messiah would declare them righteous and deserving of blessing.

143

Instead, Jesus' message to Israel was that the problem was not in the Gentile world alone. The problem, instead, was the sin inside of all people – even those of Israel. For those who considered themselves the blessed people of God, this was an offensive message. They were not acceptable to God as they were. Jesus declared that they must change.

Those of us who are Orthodox take the same offence at the suggestion that we are sinful and under God's condemnation. We, who are born and raised as members of the Church, attend our festivals, have priests to mediate for us, pray and strive to do our best – are we not favoured by God? But if the people of Israel – the nation chosen by God, the very children of Abraham through whom all blessings come – if they cannot rely on their heritage to count for salvation, then neither can we.

The Change we all Need

In AD 51 the apostle Paul travelled to Athens, to declare to them the good news of the salvation offered in Jesus alone. In a place you can still stand in today, Paul was given the opportunity to speak before the Areopagus, the philosophical guardians of the city. Before them he declared that the God, who made everything, does not live in idols or shrines. Instead, he rules over all things, and all people, and gives us life. Paul announced that this supreme creator, God, desires that people come into relationship with him.

Paul concludes by describing how this relationship can be established:

> Therefore, having overlooked the times of ignorance, God now commands all people everywhere to repent, because he has set a day when he is going to judge the world in righteousness by the man he has appointed. He has provided proof of this to everyone by raising him from the dead.
>
> Acts 17:30-31

God has been patient with humanity, and their ingratitude towards him, though he has given them everything. But the day approaches when all the world will be judged by the 'man he has appointed', namely Jesus. And, as we have seen, the whole world is guilty of rebelling against God, their maker, which in the Bible is called sin. The whole world deserves and will receive God's condemnation, and anger, unless something changes.

Paul's message, the Gospel message, declares God's judgement so we can understand the urgency, and what is at stake. However, the apostle also announces the solution: 'God now commands all people everywhere to repent'. It is the obligation on all people, everywhere, that they must acknowledge their guilt, turn their back on sin, and return to God.

Repent! It was the central message of John the Baptist. He called on all Israel to repent in order to be ready to meet God's King.[25] It was the central message for Jesus as well: 'Repent, because the kingdom of heaven has come near'.[26] God's judgement is coming for those who remain opposed to God, so repent to access the salvation that Jesus brings.

So, what does the word 'repent' mean? It translates the Greek word *metanoia* (μετάνοια) which literally means 'later knowledge'. It is the idea that, once you know the result of your actions, you will then reassess them and change your mind. Repentance is regretting your previous course of action, so that now you turn around and head the correct way.

Repentance describes all those resolutions we make after we learn through experience. Like, 'Never again will I eat a full meal just before playing 90 minutes of football', or 'In the future I will wait 24 hours before pressing send on that hastily composed angry email', or 'No more staying up all night with friends then going straight into an eight-hour workday'.

---

[25] Mark 1:4, Matthew 3:7-10
[26] Mark 1:15, Matthew 4:17

Having experienced the consequences of those actions, we resolve to never repeat them. That is repentance.

Biblical repentance takes more global effect than these examples. It is a reconsideration of the direction of your entire existence, resulting in a radical and complete life-change.

Repentance Described

1 Repentance starts with acknowledging the problem.

We can now see that the result of continuing in sinful rebellion against God will bring certain condemnation. We admit our guilt, and that we are helpless to solve the sin problem ourselves. We know we need God's mercy, so we turn away from relying on ourselves, from running our lives our own way without God.

2 Repentance then turns towards Jesus.

It recognises that only the death of Jesus in our place can save us, and his resurrection guarantees us new life. We give up our pride at thinking we could save ourselves and instead accept God's mercy in Jesus as the only way of salvation.

3 Repentance turns away from sin increasingly day by day.

For no longer do we rule our own lives, but now we live for God. God saves by ruling us, for we need to be saved from the deadly consequences of our proud independence. God progressively transforms us to grow in our hatred of sin and increase in our obedience of him.

In the 16th Century the dominant view of the solar system was of the Earth as central and stationary, orbited by the Sun and the other planets. In 1543, however, an astronomer by the name of Nicholas Copernicus published his model of a solar system, which placed the Sun in the centre around which revolved the planets, including the Earth. It was a revolutionary concept, turning upside down the dominant view of reality. Most of all, it challenged their view of themselves as the most important beings in the universe.

Even though it took a few hundred years, the model of an Earth-centred solar system was eventually abandoned. In fact, we now know that our solar system, itself, is an insignificant planetary collection on an outer edge of an average-sized galaxy, which is only one of two trillion others. The astronomical location of the Earth is not remotely remarkable – its remarkably remote.

The question of the Earth's location within the universe is no longer controversial. But, just as in Copernicus' day, we continue to think of *ourselves* as the centre of the universe. By nature, we consider that all other beings – people, and even God – revolve around us, exist to serve us. That is the very nature of sin – that our prime concern is to look after our own interests, to live for ourselves.

However, when Jesus calls on us to repent, he is proposing his own, more profound, kind of Copernican revolution. He is demanding that we open our eyes and recognise the reality that it is not we who are in the centre of the universe. That is the self-deception of sin. Repentance is to recognise the reality that the most important being in the universe is God. Repentance requires us to turn our view of reality upside down, and our lives with it. No longer are we in the centre of our lives, no longer do we live for ourselves. Now we must turn away from that lie and place God in the centre of our lives. Repentance means living to serve God.

This is not simply knowing this information about God. The Apostle James challenges us when he says, 'You believe that God is one. Good! Even the demons believe – and they shudder.'[27] They have all the knowledge about God there is to know – yet they continue to live in rebellion against him.

---

[27] James 2:19

To repent is to act on this knowledge by changing our mind about the whole direction of our life. So, repentance is not to 'turn over a new leaf', or to resolve to work harder on our spiritual journey to God. Repentance is turning away from relying on ourselves to get to God. It is to abandon our independence from God, for it only led to our destruction. It is to now submit to Jesus as our ruler, which leads us to eternal life, and to live a life now to please him.

This is not about us having to meet a standard of performance or express enough regret before God will accept us. Jesus' death is all that anyone needs to clean us completely. Repentance is our way of accepting this great gift of forgiveness, as we turn away from sin and turn towards Jesus. Or put another way, God takes us as we are, *but he does not leave us as we are.* God rescues undeserving sinners, but he calls on us to change, and he transforms us to become more like him daily.

> Repentance is a great mercy, a divine gift; for by it we are healed and saved, by it we are loosed from the chains of sin. Through repentance, we are reconciled with God and restored to his grace.
>
> Cyprian of Carthage (d AD 258)
> *Treatise on the Lapsed, Chapter 36.*

The Urgency to Turn Back

At 9.27 pm on a foggy January 5th, 1975, the bulk carrier *Lake Illawarra* collided with several pylons of the Tasman Bridge,which stretched over the Derwent River in Hobart, Tasmania, Australia. As a result, a 45-metre (150 feet) section of the bridge collapsed, falling onto the ship and into the river.

There were no cars on the collapsed section but, in the darkness, the cars that approached could not see the gap. Three cars drove over the edge, falling the 45 metres to the river, killing their occupants. Two other vehicles managed to see the gap at the last moment and screeched to a halt, front wheels teetering over the brink.

Having narrowly avoided disaster, Murray Ling, one of the drivers, frantically waved down two cars in an attempt to warn them of the danger. Both failed to heed his warnings, one of them swerving around him, which then plummeted to the river below. Seeing a bus approaching, a desperate Murray ran up to the driver's window and yelled, "There's a span missing!" The bus slammed into a side railing to slow its approach and came to a stop. Dozens of lives were saved.

We too have a warning that, continuing to live our lives as always have, will take us into the abyss. Like the bus, we must stop and change for our lives to be saved.

One can understand the reluctance to regard the warning from a stranger waving their arms on a dark bridge. However, we are being warned by the God who is utterly trustworthy, that we are headed for eternal destruction. Neither our good works, nor our religiosity – or even cultural loyalty – will merit us peace with God. They are dead ends that only provide us with false security. We travel along in comfort, like those in their cars on the Tasman Bridge, deceived that everything ahead will work out fine. But, once we have driven over the edge of life, it will be too late.

God urges us to turn back now. Repent. Head away from death and towards life. Do not swerve around God by ignoring him. In his generosity he has provided the only way of rescue – in Jesus. Why would you not choose life?

What that means, and how to go about making that commitment, is the subject of the next chapter.

SASHA'S STORY

My name is Sasha, and I am 53, an electrical engineer, married with two children.

I was brought up in a Macedonian Orthodox family. My father had a deep reverence for the tradition of our religion, and made sure we attended church during Easter, Christmas, and any other significant event in our family, such as baptisms, marriages and deaths.

The Orthodox church, for me, was an important place where I gathered with my friends, to meet girls, and connect with the traditions revered by my parents. Yet I never recall having read the Bible.

As a child I remember the day I realised that everyone dies. I lay in bed crying at the thought that my family, and me, would one day be no more. I wondered what the meaning of life could be.

After my dad committed suicide when I was 14, I took on the responsibility of providing for the family. My life was filled with work and school. I felt a deep emptiness in my life and looked for something to fill it.

I worked 12-hour shifts, seven days a week for a year, for the sports car that I thought would give me meaning. Yet, when the day came and I parked it in my driveway, I burst into tears for it had not filled the emptiness in my heart.

In my search for self-fulfilment, I tried changing my appearance. I lost weight, underwent two nose jobs, but remained unhappy. I turned on my mother for bringing me into this world, but I realised I was wrong and had only brought her grief. I sought out a professional counsellor but could still find no answers or meaning. I thought I could be happy if I obtained a diploma, but that too gave me no joy or peace. I started drinking heavily and contemplated ending it all.

Soon after, a friend at work introduced to me the teachings of Christ. I wanted to find out more, so bought a Bible to see if what he told me was in there – and it was! I started reading the Psalms every night for, in them, I found others who had undergone pain in their life and found comfort from God. The more I read in the Bible, the more hope and purpose I discovered in life.

Another work colleague invited me to his Friday night Bible Studies. There I came to understand that Romans 3:23 was true – that 'All have sinned and fallen short of God's glory'. I knew I was dirty before God and needed to be forgiven. But I also understood how much God really loved me and gave Jesus to die my death for me. So that, even though I was so unfaithful to him and had done so many bad things, I knew that he still loved me and wanted me to be with him.

I could also see in my new Christian friends a purity, cleanness, and a light coming out of them. I started asking questions about God, and how I too could have a relationship with him, and they started revealing wonderful truths, promises, and hopes from the Bible. I wanted to have what they had.

So, one Friday night, I knew that God was calling me to make the step of faith and commit my life to him. I immediately felt joy and a burden lift off me. I was welcomed into a new family, a new life – I was born again!

Since that time, God continues to work on me, to fill my life with joy, put peace in my heart, and to serve him. At times the road gets a bit rough and rocky, but I know that he is always beside me and holding my hand. I have found my eternal father, and everything he has for me is good. He has turned my greatest weaknesses into strengths and healed my sickness.

However, my family was horrified with my decision, especially my new bride. My sweet mum turned into a person of hostility towards me, and my friends turned away. I was confused. Why would they not be happy for me? For I had changed from being hopelessly lost, angry, depressed, and confused, and now had found the true meaning of life through the Jesus, whom they all revered.

I honoured my mum's wishes to speak with our family orthodox priest. I was open to changing my views, if my errors could be shown to me from the Bible. However, he could offer no alternative answers for the Biblical word of God, did not have the same authority in his thinking as it did in mine.

My wife then organised a family intervention; one characterised by peer group pressure and shame to dissuade me from my chosen path. At this stage, the words of Jesus had never rung louder and had more meaning when he said that those who would follow him would suffer persecution. The feelings of rejection were dwarfed by the immense love I felt from Jesus, by reading his word and feeling his presence in prayer.

I understand their concern arose out of love, for they thought I had changed my religion, dishonoured the Orthodox faith, and sullied the family name. However, I had not changed my faith; I had found it. Today, after investing almost 30 years of my life following Jesus and his teaching, I have concluded that God is true, whereas people can be misled. Only God can be relied upon for the truth and to lead us into eternity.

It's shocking to me now to remember how worthless I counted my life 30 years ago. Had I ended my life then, like my dad, I would have made my bed in Hell, and missed out on all the wonderful things God had prepared for me. My wife, and many family members, have since started to follow Jesus. I am enjoying a successful career as an electrical engineer, and both my children are medical professionals. No matter who you are, know that God specialises in taking even the broken and worthless, sanding them back to bare metal, coating them with the vibrant colour of righteousness. and putting it out there for other broken ones to see – all this to showcase his glory, and testify that he is, and does, have the power to change you today!

CHAPTER TWELVE

Come and Follow

The Promise of Baptism

If your background is in Orthodoxy then, like me, you were baptised as a baby. Held in the arms of your godparents, they made promises. Three times they promised to 'renounce Satan, and all his works, and all his worship, and all his angels, and all his pomp' and three times to 'join the side of Christ'.[28] But the promises they made were not for themselves. They made them as your representative, on your behalf. They were promises that looked forward to future fulfilment in your life.

Of course, as an infant, you remember nothing of that day. You may have seen photos or videos of the event, but your permission was not sought, and you did not personally agree or commit to anything. Yet, at your baptism, your parents and godparents prayed that you would, one day, make your own those promises made on your behalf.

Today you are no longer a babe in arms. You are now able to decide for yourself about how you will live. You have heard God's declaration that we

---

[28] pp21-22 *Holy Baptism* St Andrews Orthodox Press Sydney 2008

are all sinful and headed for judgement. You have understood our need of the forgiveness that can only through Christ. In the previous chapter we saw that, to accept this mercy, we must repent. No one can rely on their heritage or religious observance – all must make a conscious decision to change.

Today is the day to fulfil your baptismal promises. Today is the day for you to make the decision yourself to renounce Satan and turn and join the side of Christ.

But what does that look like?

I like to describe following Jesus with four words:

It's **easy**, yet it's **hard**.
It's **costly**, but it's **worthwhile**.

Following Jesus is Easy

As we have already seen, Jesus came to rescue his people *completely*. We do not have to prove ourselves to obtain his forgiveness. He knows and understands our inner being, and our outer actions, better than we do ourselves. Yet he came to make peace with us, even though we are his enemies.

The cleaning of our sin by his death is also applied to his people *eternally*. So, even though in this life we will continue to sin, Jesus represents us before God and is always applying his perfect sacrifice to our account so that no further payment for our sins is required. It means there is nothing left for us to do to earn our salvation. We do not have to keep up a certain level of good performance to remain in God's good books. Those who follow Jesus are permanently right with God. We can be sure of being welcomed into eternal life – not because of our hard work, but because of Jesus' finished work.

This is true liberation. We are no longer enslaved to proving ourselves before God, for Jesus has done it all for us. That is why Jesus says:

> Come to me, all of you who are weary and burdened, and I will give you rest. Take my yoke upon you and learn from me, because I am lowly and humble in heart, and you will find rest for your souls. For my yoke is easy and my burden is light.
>
> Matthew 11:28-30

Come to him, says Jesus. He will free you from the impossible task of being good enough for God. If you follow Jesus, he takes that burden for you. Following Jesus is the welcome relief of knowing that Jesus has set you free from sin.

Following Jesus is Hard

Yet following Jesus also means a change in our lives that we will find hard.

> Then he said to them all, "If anyone wants to follow after me, let him deny himself, take up his cross daily, and follow me. For whoever wants to save his life will lose it, but whoever loses his life because of me will save it."
>
> Luke 9:23-24

The very foundation of following Jesus is to deny yourself, by putting to death your independence. All we have achieved in our efforts to save ourselves from sin has been God's condemnation. Only by giving up running our own lives, by 'losing our life', by handing it over to Jesus, can we be saved.

But giving up control can be difficult for us to accept.

If you are used to being the driver of your car, this is like handing the keys to someone else to drive, and you sitting in the passenger seat. They now decide your destination, and which way to go. No more are you relying on yourself, but you must trust someone else.

But this is a more significant exercise than handing over the steering wheel. This is more akin to submitting to surgery. I certainly do not want to scare you away from necessary procedures, but have you considered to what you are consenting? With surgery you give permission to someone to render you unconscious, then to open your body, and cut and sew inside you as required. This requires that you exhibit an enormous amount of trust in those individuals. You need to be sure they are qualified and capable, as you are entrusting them with your life.

This is what it is to follow Jesus – except he is asking us to entrust him with much more. For he doesn't want just a part of us, or just for a limited time. Jesus is asking for ownership of all of us, body and soul, now and forever. To follow Jesus is to allow him to determine our purpose, our destination, and the way we live our lives. Indeed, he will even transform our minds and eventually our bodies.

It can be difficult for us to surrender control. But what are we really giving up?

> For what does it benefit someone if he gains the whole world, and yet loses or forfeits himself? For whoever is ashamed of me and my words, the Son of Man will be ashamed of him when he comes in his glory and that of the Father and the holy angels.
>
> Luke 9:25-26

There is nothing, not even the whole world, worth losing your eternal life over. We fear the loss of control, as we believe independence is the key to us being ourselves. But Jesus assures us that, if we continue to run our own lives, we will lose ourself and our only hope before God's judgement in Jesus.

The best decision you could ever make in life is to hand over your life to Jesus. He can be completely trusted. He is our creator and provides us with all good things. He knows us, and our needs, better than we know ourselves. Only by giving Jesus control will our lives be transformed for the better, and can we look forward to eternal life.

Following Jesus is Costly

Jesus also warns that this will come at a price. We have already read about Jesus describing following him as to 'take up your cross daily' and to 'lose your life'. It will be costly to be one of Jesus' people.

Jesus tells his disciples that "You will be hated by everyone because of my name" (Matthew 10:22). The Gospel of Jesus is offensive to the world because it declares that all people are sinful, enemies of God, and deserving of judgement. So too the Gospel assertion that we are helpless and need to be rescued. This is a repellent message in a world in which independence and self-reliance are the highest virtues. Some followers of Jesus have even been killed because they loved and cared for the sick in cultures where this is despised. Those who follow Jesus stand with him, and his message, and will be persecuted for it. This will always be challenging and costly.

Following Jesus also means that everything, and everyone else in your life, comes second. That includes your family, your culture, your sport, your job, and all that you now value. While all that is good can still have a place in your life, Jesus will always come first before all the competing claims in your life.

For instance, work is a good blessing from God. However, when you follow Jesus, your career cannot come first at the expense of all else. Serving God at work means acting ethically and obeying the law as you do it; working hard and honestly for your employer, and your clients; and making your family a higher priority than your career – for all these are obeying God before anyone else. Following Jesus means taking up your cross daily and putting him first always.

Following Jesus is Worthwhile

Yet ultimately, no matter the cost, following Jesus is absolutely worth it.

Living life serving God is the best way to live. He is, after all, our creator. He designed us and knows how best we operate. To grow in obedience to him is not limiting, its liberating. A derailed train will only be liberated to move, as it was made to do, when it is placed back upon its tracks. In the same way God liberates us from our sinful disobedience to become the people he designed us to be. We are transformed into people who serve him. Living God's way is the way our life works best. It is a life of meaning and purpose.[29]

Following Jesus unites you with a new community, a new family of brothers and sisters in Christ. These are people who will help you to know God better, as together you learn more about God in his word. God gives us one another, to support and encourage us along the way, in good times and bad. You will not be alone.

Most importantly Jesus gives his salvation to all who follow him. Secure and certain, nothing is more valuable than a sure eternity. Even if it means facing the disapproval of those closest to us, a loss of popularity or status, the shunning by our community, or the threat of gaol or even

---

[29] More on this in Chapter 14

physical harm. The eternal life that Jesus guarantees is worth much more than all that.

> Don't fear those who kill the body but are not able to kill the soul; rather, fear him who is able to destroy both soul and body in Hell.
>
> Matthew 10:28

Today is the Day

Where is your thinking now? What has been your assessment of this Gospel of God:

1. God made us and owns us.
2. We have all rebelled against God.
3. We deserve to be shut out from God's blessings forever.
4. God sent Jesus to die to completely rescue us from judgement.
5. God raised Jesus to life again to guarantee our eternal life.

Maybe you are still uncertain about some of these.

Here is a prayer you can pray right now. Stop what you are doing, remove yourself from any distractions, and pray these words as your own. God will hear them and has promised to answer.[30]

> Dear God. Thank you for your words that have been given to me. However, I am still uncertain. Please convince me of what is true so that I can live the life you made me to live. Amen

---

[30] Now if any of you lacks wisdom, he should ask God—who gives to all generously and ungrudgingly—and it will be given to him. (James 1:5)

However, maybe as you read the summary above, you agreed with them all. You are now convinced that God has spoken the truth: that only through following Jesus can anyone be rescued from sin and death.

Then today is the day for repentance. Today is the day to make the change, from running your life your own way, to a life where Jesus comes first. Today is the day because we do not always get a tomorrow. Today is the day because why not begin the best way to live as soon as possible?

If you are ready to make this change, here is a prayer you can pray right now. God will hear you and has promised to answer. "If we confess our sins, he is faithful and righteous to forgive us our sins and to cleanse us from all unrighteousness" (1 John 1:9).

Stop what you are doing, remove yourself from any distractions, and pray the following words as your own.

> Dear God. I am sorry that I have run my life my own way. I am sorry that I have been ungrateful for all you have given me. I am a sinner who deserves judgement.
> Please forgive me.
> Please give me confidence that, by Jesus' death in my place, he has now rescued me. Thank you that I can look forward to being welcomed, by you, into eternal life. Please change me to grow in my obedience to you daily. Amen.

If you have prayed this prayer sincerely then know that God has embraced you as one of his people. You are forgiven. Your sins have been washed away and, once and for all, Christ has made you clean. Jesus has set you free from striving to be good enough for God. You no longer need to fear giving an account of your life before God, for he will welcome you into his Heaven. We may not meet this side of eternity but, when we do,

I will be excited to meet another Orthodox believer. Your life has changed and will continue to be transformed for the better.

One final thing. You will need help in your new life. Chapter 17 has some guidance to help you in your next steps.

CHAPTER THIRTEEN

Putting Good in its Place

I would not be surprised if quite a few of you have been reading this book so far with a nagging question growing in your minds. Many of us find the idea that salvation comes entirely from God, and not at all from us to be unjust. As I discussed earlier in 'A Word about Justice', we all have an intrinsic view of justice, where evil should be punished and good rewarded – and we saw that God agrees. So, we revolt at the idea of cheap forgiveness. It seems wrong to us that the worst of the worst would be admitted to Heaven. Or that someone might live an evil life and then turn to God for forgiveness on their deathbed. How does this fit with God's idea of justice? Surely God must expect us to contribute good works to our salvation? Surely God picks those who are deserving, on whom he will confer his favour? What place, if any, do good works have in the life of the follower of Jesus?

Wages and Gifts

Around 2,000 BC, God chose a man from a backwater of Mesopotamia called Abraham. God promised that Abraham would have many descendants, that he would be blessed by God and, through Abraham, the entire world would be blessed. It was with great pride that Israel traced their line from the man blessed by God, Abraham.

So, what was his experience of relating to God?

> What then will we say that Abraham, our forefather according to the flesh, has found? If Abraham was justified by works, he has something to boast about – but not before God. For what does the Scripture say? "Abraham believed God, and it was credited to him for righteousness."[31]
>
> Romans 4:1-3

The apostle Paul suggests it would be so impressive if Abraham was good enough to earn his salvation from God, that he would be able to boast to others about it. However, that is not how the Bible describes it. Abraham was not favoured by God as a payment for good work – God *credited* him with righteousness. He did so because Abraham believed in him.

However, Abraham trusting God is not seen here as a good work that God is rewarding. Instead, a contrast is being drawn between good works and God's gift. It comes down to where someone puts their confidence. Abraham was not putting his confidence in *himself* to earn his salvation; he was putting his confidence in *God*. That is what it means to believe or have faith in God – it is to trust God with our lives. So, trusting God means believing him when he says he will save us. It is the way to accept God's gift of salvation.

---

[31] Genesis 15:6

Therefore, salvation cannot be both earned, as well as a gift. For earning something and being given something are two very different things.

> Now to the one who works, pay is not credited as a gift, but as something owed. But to the one who does not work, but believes on him who justifies the ungodly, his faith is credited for righteousness.
>
> Romans 4:5

The usual pattern of employment is that you work, in exchange for a reward, a wage. When you get paid by your employer your agreed amount of remuneration, they cannot trumpet their outstanding generosity towards you. You have earned it – you deserve the payment for which you have exchanged your time, effort, and expertise.

But conversely, what if you received a gift of $1,000 worth of tech stocks for Christmas – and the very next day those stocks increased in value by one hundred times. You could not legitimately go to each of your friends and brag about the wise investment you had made. As it was a gift, you could not even hold it up as a reflection of your wonderfulness as a person. Instead, the appropriate response would be to thank the giver profusely, and to publicly praise their generosity.

Salvation is not earned; it is given by God. The point Paul is making is that not even great Father Abraham, religious patriarch of all God's people, was considered 'right' with God because he was so good he deserved it. He too received salvation as a gift from God. The same is true for everyone. This has always been the Biblical pattern.

Salvation is for Undeserving People

When Jesus was crucified, two others were executed with him. One of them scorned and abused Jesus. He mocked Jesus, saying if he was truly the Messiah, he would save all of them.

But the second criminal reprimanded the first.

> "…Don't you even fear God, since you are undergoing the same punishment? We are punished justly, because we're getting back what we deserve for the things we did, but this man has done nothing wrong."
>
> Luke 23:40-41

This is not a nice man. He admits he is not an innocent victim. He has been found guilty of a capital crime, perhaps for what we would call terrorism, most likely for a violent crime involving taking life. He knows that soon he will be appearing before God to give an account of his life, and he knows God will find him guilty, and deserving of condemnation. There is only one hope for him.

> Then he said, "Jesus, remember me when you come into your kingdom."
>
> Luke 23:42

He took the only option any of us have. He admitted his guilt. He recognised he fell short of God's standards. Then, unlike the first criminal, he recognised that Jesus was the sinless Messiah. He accepted that Jesus was God's special anointed King, come to rescue a people into his Kingdom. He understood that his only hope was to throw himself down before King Jesus and beg for his mercy.

What was Jesus' response? Did Jesus ask the man if he had been baptised? Did he enquire about his religious instruction? His adherence to the commandments? His charitable work? He didn't have to. Anyone could see that this man was the worst of the worst. No one deserved God's favour less than this man.

Yet what does Jesus say to him?

> Truly I tell you, today you will be with me in paradise.
>
> Luke 23:43

Jesus makes this promise to this most undeserving of men. His crimes had earned him execution, and his death is certain. But so is his salvation. Jesus himself will welcome him into eternal life. Not because this man has lived a good life. No one could think that he earned his forgiveness by good works. But he will enter paradise because Jesus is now taking the punishment that this man deserves. The irony of the other criminal's call to Jesus to save them all, is that Jesus is doing precisely that – not by coming down off the cross – but by staying on it and dying for them.

Heaven will *not* be full of good people. It will be full of sinners. No-one but people who do not deserve to be there. Murderers, thieves, terrorists. Even people like you and me. No one will be there based on having qualified for their salvation or even having contributed to it by their good deeds. Yet the forgiveness of all who are gifted eternal life will not have been cheap. It will have been bought at the cost of the priceless sacrifice of Christ.

> And we, therefore… are not justified of ourselves or by our wisdom or insight or religious devotion or the holy deeds we have done from the heart, but by that faith by which almighty God has justified all men from the very beginning
> Clement, Bishop of Rome (96AD),
> *The Letter of the Church of Rome to the Church of Corinth* 32:4

This all reinforces what we saw earlier in Part 2. Forgiveness of sins is entirely the work of Jesus on the cross. Jesus is our great High Priest, forever applying his perfect sacrifice in our name before God. The resurrection of Jesus guarantees us eternal life. We can be certain because all of salvation depends on God. It is the consistent message from God in the Bible. We cannot save ourselves; we cannot contribute; we can do nothing to aid our salvation. God does not wait for us to purify ourselves so that he can reward us. And that is wonderful news, for we could never be worthy, or pure enough, and no matter how small the task was left to us, we would fail. But thanks be to God, he graciously comes to us and rescues us. It is a *gift*, not a wage. And because it relies entirely on him, we can be sure he will succeed in saving us.

The Order is Wrong

So where does that leave us with our question about the place of good works?

> For you are saved by grace through faith, and this is not from yourselves; it is God's gift – not from works, so that no one can boast. For we are his workmanship, created in Christ Jesus for good works, which God prepared ahead of time for us to do.
>
> Ephesians 2:8-10

As we have seen, God does not save people as a reward for good works. God welcomes people into relationship with him by grace – by his gift. Only subsequent to making peace with them does God transform them into a people who serve him. The good works God plans for us come *after* he saves us.

The order here is critical. Good works do not reconcile a person to God. Instead, a person who has been reconciled to God will respond with good works. In other words, you cannot earn forgiveness from God; but having been forgiven, it is right and necessary to respond in gratitude with obedience, with good works.

To illustrate I will pose you a real-life riddle. I have lived in the same home with a woman for almost forty years. We have raised five children together. We have joint finances and take holidays together. I buy her gifts on special occasions, and she does the same for me. Here is the question – what is our relationship?

I expect most of you would say we were married – but why? All these things could occur within the boundaries of other relationships. The woman could be my mother, my sister, or even a housemate. The behaviours listed here cannot *create* a marriage. However, the very reason someone might think we were married is that these are the very behaviours that you would expect *after* someone was married. The order is crucial. You cannot create a relationship by your behaviour, but you can reflect a relationship in the way you behave.

So too with our relationship with God. Good works do not create peace with God. In fact, it would be absurd to suggest that it was so. Imagine if the woman in the above example was, indeed, my housemate. Then one day after those forty years, my housemate announced to me that she had met someone, and they were planning to marry. Could I then object to her marriage by suggesting that, after sharing a house as friends for so many years, I considered we were now married? It would be a ridiculous suggestion.

But when we assume that God should be pleased and reward our good works with relationship with him, we move beyond the absurd into the offensive.

You may recall, when we looked the subject of justice, that we saw that God could not be bribed, he could not be bought off. Yet we are trying to bribe God when we think we can so impress God with our obedience or religiosity that he will look the other way when it comes to judging our case. Do we really think that God will overlook all our life of sin because we offer a few moments of good behaviour? It would be like the Mafia funeral where the hitman delivers flowers. What should the wife of the deceased think of that? "Well, he did murder my husband in cold blood but look – white roses – my favourite! I suppose he isn't such a bad fellow after all. All is forgiven." Not only would such a small amount of good never make up for all the bad, but it's also actually offensive to think someone can be bought off so cheaply like that.

It would be like expecting our employer to be so impressed by our one hour of work, they overlook us doing any more work for the rest of the week. In fact, it is worse – it would be like asking our employer for extra pay because we actually did some of the work we were already paid to do! God has given us everything in our very existence, including our lives. Even if we gave him all of ourselves, and obeyed him perfectly, we would still only be giving God what he deserves. Jesus said: "When you have done all that you were commanded, you should say, 'We are unworthy servants; we've only done our duty'." (Luke 17:10). Yet, even though we fail continually to do this, we think we can do the occasional good work and earn extra credit with God. Whenever we obey God, all we are doing is literally the least we can do. We have already been overpaid. We cannot make up for our chronic disobedience with sporadic moments of obedience.

It is also offensive to suggest that we could earn our forgiveness through our good works because that calls into question God's wisdom in sending Jesus to die for us. If our goodness could save us, Jesus wasted the sacrifice of his life, 'for if righteousness comes through the law, then Christ died for nothing' (Galatians 2:21).

The order is everything. Our good works cannot make peace between us and God – only the death of Jesus for us can do that. But, having received this forgiveness, we must respond in grateful service and obedience to God.

> For grace is given not because we have done good works, but in order that we may be able to do them.
>
> Augustine of Hippo (354-430AD)
> *On the Spirit and the Letter*

Good Works are evidence of Faith

However, we remain concerned. If obedience to God's law is not needed for our salvation because Jesus forgives us without it, then can we not simply accept forgiveness and live as we wish? This was a question asked right from the beginning.

> What then? Should we sin because we are not under the law but under grace? Absolutely not!
>
> Romans 6:15

The words translated 'absolutely not' (μὴ γένοιτο) mean just that – 'absolutely never ever' or 'may it never be'. The words could not be more emphatic. It is incomprehensible that, having been saved, you should continue to sin. For Jesus comes to rescue us from not just the penalty of sin, but from the destructiveness and damage of sin itself.

> Don't you know that if you offer yourselves to someone as obedient slaves, you are slaves of that one you obey – either of sin leading to death or of obedience leading to righteousness?
>
> Romans 6:16

By definition, sin is living independently from God. The natural state into which we are born is one of being independent from God. We are obedient to our self-interest, to doing what seem right in our own eyes. This is the definition of sin and, by nature, we are thereby in slavery to it.

But through Christ, God liberates his people from sin. He transforms those who used to serve themselves into those who now serve and obey him. Those who follow Jesus are therefore his servants; they are slaves to righteousness.

This is why it is a nonsense to suggest that those, who are saved by grace, can then choose to live as they like. We have not been liberated by Christ to serve ourselves – in fact, that is the very thing from which we have been freed – sin is doing as you please. Instead, our ownership has been transferred. No longer do we belong to Satan, sin, and death, but now we are owned by Christ, righteousness and life. There are no other choices. Bob Dylan accurately reflected the Biblical view when he wrote: 'Well, it may be the Devil or it may be the Lord, But you're gonna have to serve somebody'.

The letter of James frames the relationship of works to salvation in a different way. He says,

> ...faith, if it does not have works, is dead by itself,
>
> James 2:17

Putting your trust in God is not enough. It must be accompanied by works. He explains further:

> But someone will say, "You have faith, and I have works." Show me your faith without works, and I will show you faith by my works.
>
> James 2:18

James is saying what Paul is saying – faith is demonstrated by works. The one who trusts in God must live out a changed life. They cannot continue living as before but must now increasingly grow in their obedience to God.

> Those who profess to be Christ's will be recognised by their actions. For what matters is not a momentary act of professing, but being persistently motivated by faith
>
> Ignatius of Antioch (AD 35-107),
> *Letter to the Ephesians, 14:2*

Earlier we considered that, just because you do all the things a married couple might be expected to do together, does not make you married. But let us now think about the opposite situation. A couple stand together before a marriage celebrant. They make the usual promises to love one another in an exclusive relationship throughout all the challenges of life. The celebrant ends by declaring them husband and wife. The man and woman turn to one another, shake hands, walk out of separate doors, and never see one another again.

Are they married? Of course not! And entire departments of immigration, devoted to validating marriages, would label it as the sham it was. The promises are meaningless if they are not acted out. If you are truly married, you cannot continue to live the two separate individual lives you did before – your lives must change. The same is true of our relationship with God. Committing to following God must involve us turning our back on our independence and, instead, living for him. His great love in rescuing us ought to drive us to serve him in gratitude. The resultant good works will give evidence – not of what we have achieved – but of what God has done to secure our salvation.

> Therefore, let us not be ungrateful for his kindness. For if he were to reward us according to our works, we would cease to be.
>
> Ignatius of Antioch (AD 35-107),
> *Epistle to the Magnesians, Ch. 5*

Jesus declared that second criminal, crucified next to him, as forgiven. That criminal's ownership, at that moment, was transferred from sin and death to righteousness and life. His life was changed and, from then on, he would live in service and obedience to Jesus. The remainder of his earthly life was short. Yet, despite his painful death, though he could have responded with bitterness at God and the world like the first criminal, he instead publicly defended and declared Jesus as his rightful master. Had he survived his crucifixion, he most certainly would have lived a new life, radically different from his old one. How can I be sure? Because Jesus tells us he had rescued him – and no one can stay the same once that is a reality.

Yes, good works have a place. But it is not so we might make ourselves right with God or contribute to that result. It is not so we can show ourselves as worthy of God's grace, for none of us deserve it.

But nor is there no place for obedience. We cannot simply accept the gift of forgiveness then return to sin. Once we turn to God we turn our back on our old life of sin. Following God means being enslaved to him. And, as his slaves, we strive to serve and obey him.

In our next chapter we will see why this slavery to God is where we will find true freedom and abundant life.

CHAPTER FOURTEEN

Life to the Full

"Thou hast made us for thyself, O Lord, and our heart is
restless until it finds its rest in thee."
Augustine of Hippo, *Confessions*

FOMO and death bed conversions

Long before the term FOMO was coined, people everywhere experienced a Fear of Missing Out. Perhaps it didn't affect all of their lives, but they certainly felt that way towards God. They expressed it by assuming a life serving God is somehow impoverished, worse than living for yourself. I have had conversations with many people who have been attracted to salvation in Christ, yet have stated: "I won't become a Christian now, but I'll wait until I'm older, or even until my final breath". When pressed they will all admit that their reluctance arises from not wanting to give up their particular lifestyle choices. For them God is a spoilsport who is against fun, and living for him is dull and flavourless, without excitement or joy.

In Australia we have the term 'Wowser'. It is a label applied to anyone who censors any behaviour that they deem to be immoral or sinful. It was once suggested that Wowsers were motivated by 'the sneaking suspicion that, somewhere, someone was having fun'. That is how God is considered – the ultimate anti-fun Wowser. Living as a Christian is therefore seen to be a deficient way to live, a missing out on life.

The Good Life

The claim of God is that the opposite is true. We think we know best, but our knowledge of ourselves remains limited. We think we can make objective decisions about the right course of actions, but our motivations are clouded by self-interest. "The heart is more deceitful than anything else," says Jeremiah.[32] To live for yourself, thinking you know best, will only lead to ruin.

In the last chapter we looked at how the apostle Paul explained that, returning to sin was inconceivable for those who now followed Christ. In that same passage he appeals to his readers on this basis:

> For when you were slaves of sin, you were free with regard to righteousness. So what fruit was produced then from the things you are now ashamed of? The outcome of those things is death.
>
> Romans 6:20-21

Running our lives as we see fit is what made a mess of the world in the first place. We have destroyed ourselves, each other, and the world. We have cut ourselves off from God. All we achieved with our sin was death.

---

[32] Jeremiah 17:9

So why, asks Paul, would you want to turn back to living life for yourself? What was appealing about that when it led to death? It would be like the person who had died being brought back to life, only for them to jump back into the coffin. For, through Christ, God has offered to set us free from living for ourselves.

> But now, since you have been set free from sin and have
> become enslaved to God, you have your fruit, which results
> in sanctification – and the outcome is eternal life!
>
> Romans 6:22

God is our good creator. He knows us inside and out. Only he can provide the instructions for a life that works now, and for the eternal life to come. Far from being a spoilsport, God rescues us from our self-destructive behaviour by showing us the way to the good life and warning us of the danger of ignoring him.

The writers of the Old Testament praise God for his laws:

> The instruction of the Lord is perfect,
> renewing one's life
> the testimony of the Lord is trustworthy,
> making the inexperienced wise.
> The precepts of the Lord are right,
> making the heart glad;
> the command of the Lord is radiant,
> making the eyes light up.
> The fear of the Lord is pure,
> enduring forever;
> the ordinances of the Lord are reliable
> and altogether righteous.

They are more desirable than gold –
than an abundance of pure gold;
and sweeter than honey
dripping from a honeycomb.
In addition, your servant is warned by them,
and in keeping them there is an abundant reward.

Psalm 19:7-11

Wisdom is understanding how the world works and living in harmony with it and with each other. This knowledge is the key to a successful life, and God reveals it to us. God is our manufacturer, and the Bible is his handbook. How perfectly does God understand life, exclaims the Psalmist. How wonderful, how valuable it is to us to know this, and to follow his instructions for the good life.

The Queen of Sheba Agrees

One could, of course, accuse the people of God of being biassed. Perhaps they were simply interested in taking credit and boasting that their way of life was best.

The Queen of Sheba ruled a wealthy Kingdom in what is now modern-day Yemen. She was an outsider who makes an appearance in the Biblical narrative around 950 BC when she paid a visit to King Solomon of Israel.

The queen of Sheba heard about Solomon's fame connected with the name of the Lord and came to test him with difficult questions.

1 Kings 10:1

What the Queen had heard about Israel had piqued her curiosity. Something was happening there that was so radically different to anything else in her experience of the world, that she would make the lengthy trip of over 2,000km (1,200 miles) to see it for herself.

While we know little about Sheba, we do know about the character of the world in which the Queen lived. In the ancient world the value of your life depended on who you were. Whether you had power or wealth or had neither; if you were male or female, adult or child, healthy or sick, free or slave. The less valuable and powerful, the easier to exploit, and the more disposable. Infanticide was common and acceptable. The ancient Spartans even had a state-run system of culling their babies, where they would present their newborns to a council of inspectors, and all those deemed to have defects were abandoned to die. Societies like the ancient Canaanites would offer their children as sacrifices to appease their gods. The poor and the sick were expendable. Life was cheap. Impartial justice was non-existent.

The values of our present world are not very different but only expressed in various ways. Power, wealth, gender, age and race can still determine your value. So too can how much you can contribute to society. It can then be argued that the elderly, the young, and the disabled, become more dispensable than others. Justice for us can also be hard to find.

But, what the Queen of Sheba discovered in Israel was radically different.

> When the queen of Sheba observed all of Solomon's wisdom, the palace he had built, the food at his table, his servants' residence, his attendants' service and their attire, his cupbearers, and the burnt offerings he offered at the Lord's temple, it took her breath away.
>
> She said to the king, "The report I heard in my own country about your words and about your wisdom is true.

But I didn't believe the reports until I came and saw with my own eyes. Indeed, I was not even told half. Your wisdom and prosperity far exceed the report I heard. How happy are your men. How happy are these servants of yours, who always stand in your presence hearing your wisdom."

1 Kings 10:1, 4-8

The Queen was greatly impressed by what she saw. However, it was not the Temple or other great buildings, or the prosperity – she was so wealthy she brought and gifted 4½ tons of gold to Solomon. It was not a powerful army, or natural beauty, that caught her eye. It was the nature of their society. It was their happiness, their contentment. It was their peace with God. It was the wisdom of their laws.

She sounds like the adventurer who, today, travels to the 'Blue Zones' peoples to find the secrets to a long and happy life, and excitedly shares it with everybody. In God, and his people, the Queen of Sheba had discovered the secret to living the best life.

She specifies to Solomon what impressed her:

"Blessed be the Lord your God! He delighted in you and put you on the throne of Israel, because of the Lord's eternal love for Israel. He has made you king to carry out justice and righteousness."

1 Kings 10:9

It was the justice and righteousness she saw in Israel which the Queen found so remarkable. Righteousness is acting morally correctly, in obedience to God, and in being right with him. As we looked at in 'A Word About Justice', justice is treating others equally, fairly, and impartially.

God is the one who should be praised for all this, concludes the Queen. These ideas of justice and righteousness come from him. And, even though wise Solomon oversees this impressive society, yet it is God who appointed him.

The very values on which Israel was based stood out in stark contrast to her experience of the world. Yet, once the Queen observed them in operation, rather than reject them as strange, they immediately seemed right to her. She could see that they made sense of the world and treated people as they were created to be treated.

So, what was it about justice and righteousness that the Queen of Sheba saw? Why did she conclude that God's instructions for life are so much better than those of anyone else?

God Made All People Inherently Equal

From the very beginning of the Bible, God declares that all humans are made in his image.[33] Value is not performance based; it cannot be improved upon or lost. All people share equal dignity and must be valued by all.

The implications of this fundamental fact are many. Children are to be valued, loved, and protected. They may be small, and require resources for their care, but human-worth is not about how much one can contribute. The poor are to be fed, the sick nursed, elderly cared for, widows supported, and orphans adopted.[34] The vulnerable are not to be exploited or cheated.[35] People are not to be discarded simply because they cannot do anything for you.

---

[33] Genesis 1:27
[34] Exodus 22:22; Leviticus 25:35-38
[35] Proverbs 20:23, 22:22-23; Exodus 22:21

Humans are not to be murdered.[36] All people have inherent value as God's image-bearers. Their lives are to be protected. It is God who commands that guardrails be placed around the edge of every roof.[37] All consumer protections arise out of the inherent human value that God declares.

Because all people are equal, they all should receive the same access to justice and treatment under the law. Our western justice systems have adopted God's principles,[38] even if imperfect in their practice. It's why we have uniform laws. It's why everyone should receive a fair and impartial trial, even when it is the government that is charging them. It is why they are presumed innocent, and why they are entitled to legal representation.

God commands that punishment should fit the crime. That is a uniquely Biblical principle. There are still many cultures at present where, for instance, thieves are punished with the removal of a hand. But God says an eye for an eye, and a tooth for a tooth, as a statement of the *limits* of punishment.[39] You cannot take an eye for a tooth – that is a punishment in excess of the crime. Neither is it mandatory, as mercy may also be shown to the offender and is commended as a reflection of the character of God.[40] For even the life of a perpetrator of wrong is valuable to God.

Healthy Relationships are Fundamental

Also, at the very beginning of the Bible, relationships are at the heart of the universe. Humans have been created to relate to God, for we are made, not to be independent, but instead to rule the universe under our creator.[41]

---

[36] Genesis 9:5-6; Exodus 20:13
[37] Deuteronomy 22:8
[38] Exodus 23:6-8
[39] Exodus 21:23-25
[40] Luke 6:27-36
[41] Genesis 1:26

Humans have also been made for one another. We are not solitary and undifferentiated. We are male and female, complementary, designed to relate to each other.[42] It means that relating rightly is part of God's good design.

It also means that relating rightly to God is our most urgent need. In fact, that is why this book was written – to explain how, through Jesus, we can have certain reconciliation to God, for that is essential to living an abundant life.

These are all God Given Values

Perhaps, as you have read these paragraphs, you have thought that all these principles were obvious. Don't we all think this way about the value of human life and relationships? Are not these simply 'self-evident truths' or the 'laws of nature' as the US Declaration of Independence states? The answer is no. Much of our world does not consider such values to be the natural way to think. Without the God of Jesus Christ, we too would simply accept that 'might makes right'. We only have these notions of human worth and freedom, and all else that is good for life, because God has given them to us. The only reason we, in the western world, think this way is because those who established our laws and society inherited their ideas from a Biblical Christian worldview.

It is God who impresses upon us our need to value all the people in our lives. He gives us a responsibility to love others. It means spending time with them, prioritising their needs above ours and making other people more important than our career, sports, or hobbies. It means our marriages are the most important relationship we can have with another. It means keeping our promises to one another, being trustworthy, and faithful. It

---

[42] Genesis 1:27, 2:18-24

means honouring our parents, caring for our children, loving our friends, being generous to our neighbours, our work colleagues, our customers, and those with needs in our community and in the world. This is what makes for harmonious households and communities, and joyful lives for us all. How wonderful life would be to unconditionally love others and receive the same in return.

Perhaps this was part of what the Queen of Sheba witnessed—a people at peace with their creator. People who valued each other equally, cared for the sick, the poor, and the elderly. Who welcomed immigrants, oversaw impartial justice, loved their spouses and their families.

Yet, regarding God's design for humanity, these are just the highlights. I have not detailed how those who follow Christ are less likely to engage in self-destructive behaviours and addictions; that they are less anxious, that they are less concerned about money, and feel more at peace because they trust God. All of that is because Jesus has fulfilled his promise to us.

Jesus Offers the Abundant Life

For Jesus guarantees this to those who follow him:

> I have come so that they may have life and have it in abundance.
>
> John 10:10

This is a big claim. Jesus is saying that, only through him, can all the blessings of life be found. He alone can provide us with everything that can be gained by living life God's way. He can do that because Jesus is the only one who obeys the law completely. He fulfils the law, not only for himself, but on behalf of his people. As a result, we can share in all of the blessings that God has for us. Only through Jesus can we have certain peace with God now and into eternity, and there is nothing more valuable than that for our body, mind, and soul. But Jesus also provides us with the best life now. Following Jesus gives us the truly fulfilling and abundant life.

But there is even better news. It is not only that God reveals to us the secrets of how to live in accord with our design. He doesn't just give us a rule book, shake our hand, and wish us the best. He also changes us from the inside out so that we develop the ability to obey.

Metamorphosis

You cannot follow Jesus and stay the same. Repentance involves change, and that for the better.

> We all, with unveiled faces, are looking as in a mirror at the glory of the Lord and are being transformed into the same image from glory to glory; this is from the Lord who is the Spirit.
>
> 2 Corinthians 3:18

The word here translated transformed is *metamorphosis* (μεταμορφόομαι). Like the change of a caterpillar into a butterfly, so God does not leave us as we are, but changes us to become like Jesus. When we turn to God, he *metamorphoses* us day by day so that we become more like Jesus, his son. We become more like him in obedience to the Father, increasingly like him in right-thought and right-action. Then, when we reach our final destination in the new creation, we will be completely transformed to be like Jesus.

Dear friends, we are God's children now, and what we will be has not yet been revealed. We know that when he appears, we will be like him because we will see him as he is

1 John 3:2

Until then, God sends us his Spirit to help us grow in obedience, to our benefit.

Now the works of the flesh are obvious: sexual immorality, moral impurity, promiscuity, idolatry, sorcery, hatreds, strife, jealousy, outbursts of anger, selfish ambitions, dissensions, factions, envy, drunkenness, carousing, and anything similar. I am warning you about these things – as I warned you before – that those who practice such things will not inherit the kingdom of God. But the fruit of the Spirit is love, joy, peace, patience, kindness, goodness, faithfulness, gentleness, and self-control.

Galatians 5:19-23

All of us are born in sin, acting as we think best, living for ourselves. We engage in self-indulgent and ultimately self-destructive behaviours. Not only do they result in God's condemnation and eternal death, but they are behaviours that are detrimental to others, as well as to ourselves. Only through supernatural intervention, through the Spirit of God, can we be empowered by God to change for the better. God transforms his people, in increasing measure, to adopt these fruits of the Spirit. All of them are positive, serving God and others instead of ourselves, and also for our best.

The Joy of Obedience

I have a double reason to bristle at the concept of submitting to God in obedience. Like everyone else I was born a sinner, so my nature is to want to resist God, and live independently of his control. But I was also born an Australian and we are, by culture, anti-authoritarian. We take pride in being able to do things ourselves and look down on those who need help. We are also cynical of the abilities and motivations of those who would desire to lead us.

However, following Jesus must be about change. It is about turning our back on our disastrous life of sin, which leads only to death and, instead, embrace the abundant life that Jesus offers. It is about recognising that God is our creator and entirely good, so that what he commands for us is for our best. That should excite us to learn the secrets to successful life that come from obeying our maker.

Therefore, our response should not be that we begrudgingly do the minimum God requires of us to be counted as obedience. That is what you do when you doubt the goodness of the one who commands you. This is when you are convinced that God is against you, and you only obey to avoid punishment. This is what motivated the Pharisees and still motivates many religious people today.

Instead, if we recognise that God is offering the best life, we should seek to find out as much as we can about how we work best. We should search out God's commands and seek to obey them to the fullest. If you were offered an investment that was guaranteed to double your money, you would invest all that you have. God offers us a far better return than that if we serve him – so why wouldn't we obey?

This is not to say that every day will be puppies and rainbows, and everyone will smile at us. No, for we continue to live in a world tainted by sin. We will continue to fail God, ourselves, and one another. There will still be suffering and evil that will spoil life. In fact, all will suffer *more* because they follow Jesus, not less. Yet, to serve him is *still* the best life, the abundant life. Jesus restores our relationships with God, with each other, with the world, and with ourselves. God tells us how relationships work best, how we ought to conduct our marriages, warns us against addictive substances that will harm our bodies, guides us in wisely stewarding our money, teaches us how to love one another, commands us to care for his creation, and teaches us to work diligently. And he transforms us so we can obey. This is living as we were created to be.

Serving our God is the key to loving life and seeing good days.

> Finally, all of you be like-minded and sympathetic, love one another, and be compassionate and humble, not paying back evil for evil or insult for insult but, on the contrary, giving a blessing, since you were called for this, so that you may inherit a blessing.
>
> For the one who wants to love life
> and to see good days,
> let him keep his tongue from evil
> and his lips from speaking deceit,
> and let him turn away from evil
> and do what is good.
> Let him seek peace and pursue it,
> because the eyes of the Lord are on the righteous
> and his ears are open to their prayer.
> But the face of the Lord is against
> those who do what is evil.
>
> 1 Peter 3:8-12

Why wouldn't we want to invest our whole lives with a God like this?

> Come to me, all of you who are weary and burdened, and I will give you rest. Take my yoke upon you and learn from me, because I am lowly and humble in heart, and you will find rest for your souls. For my yoke is easy and my burden is light.
>
> Matthew 11:28-30

GEORGE'S STORY

My name is George Vassilopoulos. I'm 56 years old, married with three adult children, and work as a financial adviser.

Being the first son of a Greek migrant family, I took for granted that being Greek was being Orthodox, and that meant we try to reach God in a mystical way. It always struck me that my father's brother, who was outwardly ignorant of the world and immoral, knew the 'evil eye' so, whenever I was sick, he would chant and I would get better! Why did God listen to him? Superstition best described my understanding of Greek Orthodox faith.

But my parents weren't united in religion. My mum was sent to Australia by her dad to find a better life. When they parted my granddad said to her: "I have nothing to give you but my New Testament, read it because it contains the word of life".

In my teens, mum revealed she had come to believe in Jesus. She and dad fought over that a lot. It was a disgrace for my dad. In public, my mum was known as a heretic, called 'heterodox' by our relatives and friends.

Personally, my faith was in partying and hedonism. That was instant and tangible. Reaching out in blind ignorance held no interest for me. None of that would get me high. There was nothing long term, in my vision. I don't remember fear of the unknown, or of death. The only concern I had was when the party ended.

The problem was, there was a growing emptiness that accompanied my lifestyle. So I worked harder at more partying and excess. That only increased the emptiness.

In those days, I remembered my mum's words about God, that he is real, that he is there. I was desperate to deal with the horrible emptiness that I couldn't fill. I was also feeling dirty inside, and a guilt I couldn't explain. One day I asked God for help while preparing to go out. Instantly, I felt a presence that was so real, I even said 'but not tonight, God'. Yet that night I met someone who told me they shouldn't be there because they were Christian – our conversation lasted hours, and we met the next day to go to a church where his dad was pastor.

I clearly remember the message he delivered from Mark 4:34 – 'Jesus calmed the storm for the disciples, and he can calm the storm in your life also'.

That was February 4, 1990. After those days, people taught me about Jesus, and I continue to follow him now.

When I started following Jesus, I thought I was being faithful to Orthodoxy since, in my simple thinking, I was serving Jesus as God. Unfortunately, our local priest felt differently and, on one visit to our home, he cursed my mother as the one to blame for my heretical conversion. When I challenged him with the Bible, he spat on me as he left.

Since those early days, I have found that the enemy is not the priests, or the Orthodox faith, but my own sinful tendencies which war against everything God wants for me and has for me.

These days, I am still amazed how real Jesus is in my life, and how he manages to communicate his unconditional love. It's opposite to the empty, blind, supernatural reaching out in a vague attempt for God's favour – he reaches out despite my blindness and literally brings me life. Instead of my independence sprinkled with occasional traditions, I am called to a constant, unceasing walk with him. I find myself yearning to be with him and see him tangibly – it's always been about the instant tangible for me, so I struggle with the wait for Heaven and my constant failures before a pure, perfect, and incredible God.

I hope we can meet in God's kingdom so I can hear your Christian story. Jesus is there.

In Matthew 11:28-29, Jesus says: "Come to me, all of you who are weary and burdened, and I will give you rest. Take my yoke upon you and learn from me, because I am lowly and humble in heart, and you will find rest for your souls."

PART 4

Where to now?

CHAPTER FIFTEEN

Welcome Home

The Failure of Transactional Relationships

We are all familiar with the concept of paid employment. Someone engages you to do a certain task, or work for an amount of time, and in return they pay you. You receive money from them, not as a gift but as something you have earned by your labour. The more you work, the more money you earn. This is an arrangement that works well for jobs.

However, when applied to personal relationships, this transactional way of thinking has disastrous consequences. Consider a parent who keeps track of all the costs of raising their child to ask them to pay them back that money when they grow up. Or a friendship, or marriage, where nothing is done for the other person unless they can do something in return.

It is a depersonalising way to be treated. People are considered to be nothing more than a balance sheet, as a debt to be paid, or a debtor to be claimed against. When you are treated in this way it brings any claim of the other's affection for you into doubt. Are they doing something for me because they like, or have concern for me, or because they want something in return? Will they stand by me through thick and thin, or will their involvement with me always be determined by what they can get out of it? Such people are only treating others as resources to be exploited, rather than valuing them as people.

That is not what characterises authentic relationships. Genuine relationships are about love for another, and of desiring to serve them. They should be characterised by giving selflessly, without counting the cost. They should be about giving because you want to give. Freed from doubts over their motives, you can truly appreciate their service to you as proof of their love for you.

The Ungrateful Son

In Chapter Three of this book, we considered a story featuring a young man who thought about his familial relationships in just such a transactional way.

You will recall that Jesus told the story of this son who demanded from his father his share of his inheritance. In other words, he declared to his father's face that he wished he were dead. He didn't want his father to interfere in his life, and he didn't thank him for what he had been given. Taking the money, he travelled as far away from home as he could, where he rapidly spent all he had received.

Facing starvation, he decided to return home. However, he did not do so out of a desire for reconciliation with his father, but only because he sought a well-paid job as one of his father's employees.

The younger son had treated his father as simply a source of money. He expressed no affection for him, and no regret at his ingratitude and betrayal of his father. Then, unsurprisingly, his solution to his problem followed the same transactional pattern. He had exhausted his money supply, so his solution was to replace it. Returning to his father and requesting a job were only a means to achieve this end. No feelings involved, it was just business. He even fashioned a little speech to manipulate his way into a job.

> ..."Father, I have sinned against Heaven and in your sight.
> I'm no longer worthy to be called your son. Make me like
> one of your hired workers."
>
> Luke 15:18-19

Here is a model non-apology. The son's goal is not to express regret, or ask for forgiveness, but to get that job.

But the son had misidentified the problem and so was seeking the wrong solution. His real problem was his broken relationship with his father. And no matter how hard he worked, or how much money he acquired, he would not be able to buy his way back into that relationship. He could not earn forgiveness. That would be a transactional way of thinking about people.

A friend of mine grew up with a short-tempered father who would frequently overreact angrily at the slightest provocation. On several occasions after his outbursts, he would buy her expensive gifts, like watches, radios, and jewellery, as compensation. He never apologised and never admitted error. He expected to be able to buy back his daughter's affection with gifts and continue to behave as he wished.

However, it was not a present that she needed. She needed him to understand that he had hurt her, to accept responsibility for that behaviour, and to endeavour to not repeat it. A gift is an attempt to distract from the problem, and a way to avoid taking blame for harm caused. You cannot pay off someone whom you have offended to compensate for the personal wounds that you have inflicted.

So how *do* you mend a broken relationship?

The Deep Compassion of the Father

It is demonstrated in the conclusion to Jesus' story as the young man returns home.

> So he got up and went to his father. But while the son was still a long way off, his father saw him and was filled with compassion. He ran, threw his arms around his neck, and kissed him.
>
> Luke 15:20

Typically, middle-eastern fathers occupy a position of dignity as respected elders within their family and community. They issue their instructions, and expect their subordinates to carry them out. They do not plough the fields, harvest the crops, or tend the flocks – they have employees to complete those tasks.

So, the last thing we would expect from such a father was for him to run. Only little boys gathered up their robes in their hands to run, for that is what you must do to avoid tripping over it. Yet this father exhibits this undignified behaviour. He is running when he has employees that could do any task for him. Imagine a President or a King running down the corridor to get some urgent photocopying done!

Added to his indignity is the reason for which he runs. He rushes to greet this son who has publicly disgraced himself. We might expect the father to have sent his servants to drive the son out of town and make clear he is never welcomed back. Yet, even though the entire town knows how this son had treated his father and his family, though they would have seen this father demean himself by running out to him, yet this man humbled himself by running out to his boy. And rather than curse and beat his son as we might expect, the original Greek says the father "throws himself on his neck and kisses him". This is an evocative image of this father embracing his beloved son with his whole being. This father does not care how he looks, or what other people would inevitably think or say about him. He only wants to express his love for his son.

The father's motivation for acting this way is described in the phrase in the middle of the verse where it says he, 'was filled with compassion'. The word translated 'compassion' (ἐσπλαγχνίσθη) is from the root word *splagchnizomai* from the Greek word *splagchnon* or gut.[43] In Greek thinking the gut was the seat of the emotions. It's why we still talk about having a 'gut feeling' and describe being anxious as having 'butterflies in the stomach'. *Splagchnizomai* describes being moved so profoundly by something that you feel it in the pit of your stomach.

This father has an intense compassion for his son that arises from deep within him, from the very centre of his being. It is a compassionate love that drove him to constantly look for his son – for that is how he sees him coming from a long way off he has been out looking for him every day. And now he demonstrates his love.

For the father understands that the real problem this son has is not hunger, or poverty, but the broken relationship with his father. He also understands that the only way to restore this man to sonship is for the father to forgive him. It is out of his compassion that the father runs to his son and pays the price of humbling himself for their reconciliation.

---

[43] Those with a background in anatomy will recognise this Greek word from the splanchnic nerves which supply the abdominal organs.

Only Forgiveness Can Heal Relationships

Then comes the son's response to his father:

> The son said to him, "Father, I have sinned against Heaven
> and in your sight. I'm no longer worthy to be called your
> son."
>
> Luke 15:21

The son cuts his original speech short, omitting the request for a job. After seeing his father's reaction to him, he now understands the real problem he is facing is not poverty. Seeing his father's tears, his compassion, his joy at being reconciled, the son now understands how he had broken his father's heart. It is in seeing his father's love that the son finally recognises and confesses his unworthiness. Only now that he has been offered his father's forgiveness does he recognise that broken relationships can only be healed when the offended party forgives the other.

The father then proceeds to put that forgiveness into action.

> But the father told his servants, 'Quick! Bring out the best
> robe and put it on him; put a ring on his finger and sandals
> on his feet. Then bring the fattened calf and slaughter it,
> and let's celebrate with a feast…'
>
> Luke 15:22-23

The father's best robe, that is reserved for special occasions and honour, is placed on the son. The fattened calf that is set aside for the most significant of celebrations, is prepared. The ring and sandals are not provided to employees. These demonstrate that the son, is once again, a member of this family. This man, who deserved only contempt and exclusion, has been completely restored as a son. Though he squandered his inheritance he has become a full family member and an heir once more.

All of this comes about only through the forgiveness of his father. The son cannot earn his restoration; he can do nothing to make his father give it. This reconciliation is affected through the father's costly demonstration of unexpected love. Not once does this father mention that the family fortune has been wasted. Not once does he ask for repayment or place any other conditions on their reuniting. This father treats his son, not with the anger the son deserves, but instead with mercy, forgiveness, and generosity.

Only God is a Father like this

Of course, Jesus constructed this story to teach us. The behaviour of this father is purposely idealised. No human father could be so tolerant, so forgiving. This father is a picture of our heavenly Father, God.

Like the younger son, we have all squandered the blessings that God has richly given us. Without thanks we all take what he has given us, and run our lives without him. We are far away from God in a distant country. We know there is a problem, but we cannot identify it nor solve it on our own.

Yet, though we are far from him, God comes to us. Jesus, both God and man, gives up his heavenly throne, and humbles himself to become one of his creatures. God became one of us, to run to us. Then, having found us, he demonstrates his deep compassion by offering us forgiveness at great cost.

Many have titled this story 'The Prodigal Son' where the word prodigal is a word meaning 'extravagant wastefulness'. Yet it should rightly be called 'The Prodigal God' for it is God's generosity to us that is without measure. It is for us that our heavenly Father spends the life of his only son; who becomes death for us so we might not have to face it; who provides it freely to all who will take it; who does not ask us to repay our debt to him, for we cannot.

But, even more than that, God welcomes us to be at home with him to be the people we were created to be – children of our heavenly Father. He transforms us from people who served themselves, to those who serve him. He adopts us as sons who can look forward to a heavenly inheritance. There he will richly bless us, without the taint of evil, forever.

This is the Father of the story Jesus told. He comes to us in a costly demonstration of unexpected love. He does so because he knows there is no other way, and he longs to restore us back to him.

Another Lost Son

However, you may be saying to yourself – I have never been wayward like this younger son. I have never betrayed anyone or spent all their money. I have always striven to fulfil what was expected of me by my family, my culture, and my God. I do not need the forgiveness the younger son needs, and I deserve better than anything that son gets. This is undoubtedly what the religious leaders thought, to whom Jesus told this story.

To them, and to us, Jesus says that there was another son.

> Now his older son was in the field; as he came near the house, he heard music and dancing. So he summoned one of the servants, questioning what these things meant. 'Your brother is here,' he told him, 'and your father has slaughtered the fattened calf because he has him back safe and sound.'
>
> Then he became angry and didn't want to go in. So his father came out and pleaded with him. But he replied to

his father, 'Look, I have been slaving many years for you, and I have never disobeyed your orders, yet you never gave me a goat so that I could celebrate with my friends. But when this son of yours came, who has devoured your assets with prostitutes, you slaughtered the fattened calf **for him**.'

Luke 15:25-30

The older son accuses his father of treating his sons unequally. His brother wasted his father's money, whereas the older brother did all he was told. So, if anyone has earned a celebratory feast, it should be the older brother, not the younger. The older son demands to receive what he has earned by his obedience.

This way of thinking about relationships should sound familiar to us. The older son had the *same* transactional view of relationships as his brother. Yes, he was obedient, but here he reveals his motivation. He had not obeyed out of respect or love for his father, but to earn his favour. The older son reasons that, as he has worked harder, he deserves more from his father.

But the father corrects the older son's view of relationships.

'Son,' he said to him, 'you are always with me, and everything I have is yours. But we had to celebrate and rejoice, because this brother of yours was dead and is alive again; he was lost and is found.'

Luke 15:31-32

The father does not pay his son's wages, like he is one of his employees. He does not feed him or clothe him or *love* him according to his work performance. He is part of his beloved family. All the members of the family share in the blessings of that family. The celebration is therefore not a celebration of the younger son's bad behaviour, or a reward for good. It is not about which son has behaved the best. Nor is it about the younger son rehabilitating himself or being honoured for having reformed his life.

The reason they 'had to celebrate and rejoice' is given in verse 32 – it was because the son was 'found'. And whilst the younger son can take the blame for becoming lost, he did not *find* himself. He was *found*. He was rescued by another.

He was found by his father who came looking for him. Found through his father's generous mercy in forgiving him and restoring him to being a son again. The fattened calf is slaughtered in verse 27, 'because he has him back safe and sound'. The party is a celebration of *the father's mercy* in rescuing his son.

The tragedy of the older son is that he refuses to enter the party. His father pleads with him and yet, as the story ends, we are left with the question – will he remain outside, or will he accept the invitation to join his family?

Which Son are You?

So, with which son do you most identify?

Some of us, like the younger son, defiantly rebel against God's authority to run our lives. Perhaps we have been angry at God, denying his existence or his goodness. We have told ourselves that we know better than God in running our lives. So we create our own rules and live the way we think best. We take pride in the fact that we are not sheep. We are independent thinkers, and do not blindly follow anyone. We tell ourselves that the good we have we have earned and deserve, and we have not freeloaded off anyone.

If that describes your life now you are far away from God. You have rejected him as your creator and provider of all good things. You have denied him the thanks and service he deserves. Your relationship with God is broken.

Some of us are more like the older son as we earnestly seek to please God. We adopt and practice what we understand of God's rules or engage in self-denial in the hope that God will be pleased with us. We take pride that we have kept the rules, respected our family, community, ethnicity, and traditions. We tell ourselves that the good we have we have earned and deserve, and we have not freeloaded off anyone.

If that describes your life now, you too are far away from God. You think your attempt to win God's favour will force him to love you. You want to earn your own way to God. Your pride is in being better than others, and your love is of your efforts instead of in your God. You think of God as a sadistic taskmaster who always demands more, instead of the loving father whose joy it is to bless us.

Like the older son, you stand outside of the party because you want to be able to merit your entry by being good enough. As a result, you reject God's forgiveness. Your relationship with God remains broken.

He who thinks he lives without sin puts aside not sin, but pardon.

Augustine of Hippo (AD 354-430) *The City of God* (Book 14 ch 9)

Different sons, same problem

The error of the sons with their father is our error in thinking about God. For all of us consider God in that same transactional way.

We treat God as if he were an ATM. We think that all we need do is input the correct code into him, the right combination of behaviour, then to us will flow his blessings. We therefore conclude that, if all is not well in our lives, then our problem with God is that we have not done enough. Like the older son in his complaint, we think everyone should receive what they deserve, according to their effort and character. We insist on justice from God – but we do not understand for what we are asking.

For like both sons, we have misdiagnosed the issue. Our problem with God is not that our work is incomplete, so that we must work harder. Our problem is the broken relationship between our Heavenly Father and us, his children.

Thankfully God does *not* give us what we deserve. For what is it we deserve? It is we who have turned our backs on God. What we *deserve* is contempt, condemnation, and exclusion from God's blessings forever.

But praise to our great heavenly Father, for instead he is kind and merciful and loves us deeply. Rather than give us what we deserve, he offers us forgiveness. He invites us to be restored into his family with all the blessings that includes. He invites us to come home.

Come home and join the Party

There is no feeling like coming to the place where you feel welcome, loved, and safe, especially when you have been far away.

When I was 23, I took my first trip overseas. I was newly married but had left my wife behind for three months in order to study. Even though it was a great adventure, it was also a time of intense homesickness. I felt alone in an unfamiliar country, with strange foods and customs.

So when, on that final Qantas flight descending over Sydney Harbour, they played 'I still call Australia home', I burst into tears (I'm crying thinking about it now!). I had been far away but had now returned to the wife and parents whom I loved, and who loved me. I was back in the place where all was comfortable and familiar, and I belonged. And we celebrated, for I was home.

God is inviting all of us to come home.

Hear what Jesus says:

Don't let your heart be troubled. Believe in God; believe also in me. In my Father's house are many rooms. If it were not so, would I have told you that I am going to prepare a place for you? If I go away and prepare a place for you, I will come again and take you to myself, so that where I am you may be also.

John 14:1-3

A place has been prepared for all those who believe – to put their lives in the hands of God. A home to live with him, forever.

God in the Bible describes Heaven as a place of 'rest'. Rest is the idea that it will be a place where good will no longer be frustrated by evil and corruption, but where the joy will be uninterrupted. No longer will people die before their time. Work will not be frustrated by having others steal it. And there will be peace. Such will be the absence of conflict that even the animals will no longer hunt one another – 'the lion will lie down with the lamb'.[44]

These ideas are picked up again in the book of Revelation:

Then I heard a loud voice from the throne: "Look, God's dwelling is with humanity, and he will live with them. They will be his peoples, and God himself will be with them and will be their God. He will wipe away every tear from their eyes. Death will be no more; grief, crying, and pain will be no more, because the previous things have passed away."

Revelation 21:3-4

God has made a home for us to share, where we can enjoy all the good blessings he has for us forever, without interruption.

---

[44] Isaiah 65:17-25

More than that, Heaven is described many times as 'a place of feasting'. The angels celebrate whenever anyone returns to God.[45] In Matthew 8:11, Jesus says:

"I tell you that many will come from east and west to share the banquet with Abraham, Isaac, and Jacob in the Kingdom of Heaven".

Then in Revelation, which looks into Heaven, we see a table and a banquet:

> Then the angel said to me, "Write this: Blessed are those
> who are invited to the wedding supper of the Lamb!"
>
> Revelation 19:9

"You are a sinner, I am a sinner. Both of us are sinners. But do you not see that he is without sin? Let us not lose heart, therefore. For we have been invited to the marriage feast, we have been invited to the kingdom of God. He who has invited us is not a person to lie; nor does he wish to disappoint his guests."

John Chrysostom (AD 347-407)

Homily on Matthew

Great will be the celebration. Finally, no more death, pain, hunger or frustration. Reunited in celebration with the people we love, and where we will be loved. We will serve God and sing His praise forever, for all his goodness towards us. We will be the human beings we were made to be. We will be experiencing a life that is eternal because it is the fulfilment, the very definition of what life is all about. We will be wholly and genuinely home.

God wants so much to welcome you home that he sent his only Son to bring you. God values you so highly that he paid the price of his Son's life to rescue you from death so you could enjoy life.

---

[45] Luke 15:10

Won't you come home to where you belong?

Then, one day in eternity, you can look forward to hearing from your heavenly Father:

> Welcome home, my lost child.
> I came in rescue of you, dear daughter.
> I paid a great price to deliver you from death, beloved son.

ANTHONY'S STORY

My parents were Greek Immigrants to Australia. They were loving, and worked hard to provide for us. I was baptised and raised Orthodox, and we celebrated Easter and occasionally attended Church, but I knew little about God, and even less about Jesus. The only lesson drummed into me was that God was a judge who would punish my every sin.

I married at the age of 21, and we had two sons. I worked long hours to provide for my family and aimed to buy three houses – one for us, and one to give to each of my sons. However, in my early thirties, my marriage began to break down. For my part, I was plagued by insecurities, I blamed my wife for everything and was unforgiving. After she started a relationship with another man, I found myself ejected from my own house and excluded from my sons' lives.

From then on all I could think about was reconciling to my wife and being with my sons. I lost weight and went to the gym. I sent gifts, and I wrote love poems to commend myself to my wife, but to no avail. In desperation I cried out to God, visited numerous Churches, and lit countless candles, then grew angry with God for not giving me back my family. I thought I was looking for justice but instead was looking for someone to blame.

Then, on one Sunday morning, I was passing a Church as it was emptying out. The attendees looked so happy, which only made me angrier with God because I was not. But I felt compelled to enter, to discover more. Seeing my stricken face, two of their members listened to my story, and spoke kindly with me. They explained how sin and Satan destroy our relationships. I accepted their invitation to return for their evening meeting.

I was suspicious. All the time I could hear in my mind my mother's words warning me about cults, reminding me that, being Orthodox, was who we were, that it was our identity. But it all sounded true to me, so I needed to hear more.

The preacher that night spoke of forgiveness. Not only did I hear how God could forgive me, but also how I could begin to forgive others. There and then I asked God for me to be forgiven. Immediately I felt incredible joy! I remember that whole week – feeling light, unburdened, and filled with thankfulness to God for all he had done for me. I had so obviously changed that my concerned parents wanted me to see a psychiatrist.

Yet I still did not fully understand what had happened to me. Soon afterwards I met George, a Greek friend from my childhood. He, too, had become a follower of Jesus. George and his wife, Anastasia, invited me into their home, and patiently explained the Gospel to me. It was then that I understood God's generosity to me was in sending Jesus to die in my place, so I could be forgiven. God had done something I did not deserve, and could never earn, something unthinkable. For while I could never give up either of my sons, yet God gave his precious Son for me.

God had not abandoned me. He always gave me someone, at the right place, and right time, to guide me into the truth. All I needed to do was submit to God, for his ways are best. I continue to struggle to obey but, over time, God is helping me become more patient and forgiving.

I am so thankful to God for how he has protected my sons and preserved my relationship with them. They have married and I now rejoice in three grandchildren. I am also friends with my ex-wife. I have re-married to a Christian woman and, with her, raised her two children. In addition, I have the benefit of being welcomed into new families of those who also follow Jesus, like George and Anastasia's.

How great is God to have forgiven me and welcomed me into relationship with him. He provided me with even more family than before! It still brings tears of joy to me today when I consider that, unworthy though I am, yet God has blessed me so richly through Jesus.

CHAPTER SIXTEEN

At the Crossroads

In my first month of practising as a doctor, I arrived for an evening shift in our busy emergency department. At the handover, we stood at the foot of one particular patient's bed. He was a man in his sixties who, over the preceding week, had been experiencing fevers, a productive cough stained with blood, and increasing shortness of breath. He was receiving a high flow of oxygen by mask, but his blood oxygen remained quite low (saturating in the 70s for those in the know). He was assured by our most experienced doctors that he was extremely unwell, and was required to be admitted for urgent care.

However, despite that, he was adamant that he would be returning home. Speaking breathlessly, a word at a time, he explained that all he came for was some antibiotics. Yet all the doctors assured him that, should he leave, he would die.

This man stood at the crossroads of his life. Would he believe the experts and submit to life saving treatment? Or would he put more confidence in his own assessment of his condition, and leave?

We have a Decision to Make

If you have read this far, and are not yet following Jesus, you now stand at the crossroads of your life. It is not concerning a physical diagnosis, but rather a much more significant spiritual one. Our diagnosis has been delivered to us by the undisputed expert in all matters human and divine, God himself, speaking to us through the Bible.

We have seen that God has delivered to all of us a devastating and unwelcome diagnosis. All of us have rebelled against him, run our own ways without God. As a result, we have messed up ourselves and one another, and the world in which we live. God loves all of us so deeply that he won't allow this state of harmful behaviour to continue. On the day he has chosen he will bring an end to the evil in our world, by submitting all of us to judgement. He warns us that we are all guilty, and all deserve destruction and banishment to Hell for eternity.

However, in his great mercy and love for humanity, God has not abandoned us. He sent his Son, Jesus Christ, to provide a rescue for us. Jesus lived the perfect life, innocent of sin and, therefore undeserving of death. However, he chose to suffer death in the place of his people. He took the white-hot anger of God that we deserved so that we will not have to. As God-become-man his life was of such great worth that, in his death, he paid the penalty of judgement, not just for one but for many. God then raised Jesus to life again to demonstrate his power over death. Through that resurrection, Jesus guarantees for us an eternal future in a glorious new creation, unspoiled by evil, death, disease, or tears. Jesus calls on us to repent – to turn away from independence from God and to come and follow him. All else must come second in our lives to service of, and obedience to, Jesus.

God leaves us with a decision to make. There is no fence to sit upon – if you do nothing then you have decided to continue living as before, independently of God.

Choosing to Stay the Same

You can choose to continue living your own way, in defiance of God. You will be depriving yourself of the best life with meaning and purpose, as only life under God can provide those. Ultimately, God assures you of death and judgement.

Perhaps it is because you remain unconvinced of all you have heard. If that is so, can I again suggest that you ask God for help? Here is a prayer you can pray now, to ask God to reveal the truth to you.

> Dear God. Thank you for your words that have been given to me. However, I am still uncertain. Please convince me of what is true so that I can live the life you made me to live. Amen

However, perhaps you know that everything we have looked at in God's word is true. You know you will face God's condemnation, and the only hope of salvation is in turning to Jesus. Yet there is something in your life that is stopping you from making the change. If this is you, ask yourself right now – what in my life is stopping me from following Jesus?

Is it fear of disapproval from your family, your friends, your community, or society as a whole? That will almost certainly happen, for the unbelieving world hates Jesus, and so hates his followers. It can be difficult. But ask yourself – is their approval more important than your eternal destiny, than escaping Hell and embracing life?

Perhaps it is fear of missing out on the 'good life'. Or you have specific lifestyle that you know you will not be able to continue as a follower of Jesus. Firstly, remember that God's way is always the best way to live. Change will not be easy, but God promises to transform us to be more like Christ daily' and he provides other believers to help us. Secondly, remember that, once again, no matter what it is, nothing is more important than avoiding God's judgement, and living for him.

Maybe you have met, or know someone in your life, who claims to be a Christian but who you feel lives a hypocritical life. Perhaps they have caused you grief and harm. I am sorry if that is the case. However, that is not an excuse for not following Jesus. For, while people will always disappoint us, Jesus never will. He is loving and deeply desires for you to come to know him, and escape judgement. Come and follow Jesus – then pray for that person in your life to also be changed by Jesus.

What is stopping you from making the change today? Is it worth giving up your soul?

> For what will it benefit someone if he gains the whole world yet loses his life? Or what will anyone give in exchange for his life?
>
> Matthew 16:26

Choosing Life

Instead, you can accept that God's diagnosis and cure for us is correct. You can make the wise choice to change and follow Jesus.

Yes, it can be costly – but it is so, so worth it. Following Jesus enables us to live life now, as we were designed to do under God – a life with meaning and purpose, forgiveness guaranteed, and life forever. We can look forward to a new resurrection body that will never break, or grieve, or be anxious, and become part of a new family with all those who serve and follow Jesus.

In the story with which we began this chapter, we left the patient contemplating a decision – should he stay in hospital or go home. Despite the experts, this man's mind was unchanged, and he discharged himself against medical advice and walked out. Minutes later a bystander ran into the emergency department to alert us that someone had collapsed on the footpath. Rushing outside with our emergency trolley, we found this poor man face down in a pool of blood. He was not breathing, he was pulseless and, despite all efforts, could not be resuscitated.

This is not a story about the infallibility of doctors. They make mistakes, as do all humans. But in this instance, the evidence was overwhelming, and their diagnosis was correct. Sadly, the patient had made the wrong choice, at the cost of his life.

The doctor of our souls, God, is never in error. Out of his love he has warned us of imminent and significant danger. Out of his love and amazing generosity, he has offered us rescue and life to the full.

Do not make the mistake of doubting God. Do not delay. We do not know when Jesus will return and bring an end to all creation. We do not know when we will die and must then give an account of ourselves to God. If you know what God declares to us is true, then accept the eternal lifesaving treatment that only Jesus offers.

If you are ready to make that change now, you can pray these words to God:

Dear God.

I am sorry that I have ignored you, and run my life my own way. I now believe what you have said – that I am a sinner who deserves judgement.

Please forgive me.

Today I come to you to begin a new life following Jesus. Please help me to grow in obedience to you daily. Please help me grow in knowledge of you. Please provide me with fellow believers to help me.

Thank you that I can look forward to being welcomed, by you, into eternal life.

Amen.

If you have prayed this prayer sincerely then know that you have made the right decision. You have come to the crossroads and have chosen Life! God has wiped your account clean of debt and declared peace between him and you.

Now is the time to start a new life. But you will need help and encouragement so you can grow in knowledge and obedience.

NIKI'S STORY

My name is Niki. I am a 63-year-old woman, of Greek-Australian background. I had a career as an educational developer in a university and, while now in retirement, I care for my elderly relatives and my baby great-nephew.

When I was a small child, the highlight of my week was to attend Sunday School at my local Orthodox Church. However, by the time I had reached my mid-teenage years, I had begun to question everything about my religion. I don't recall being taught anything about what Jesus had done for me. It was just a set of rituals and religious practices that I didn't understand. My parents could not answer my questions so, by the time I had become a young adult, I rebelled against what I regarded as 'old-fashioned superstitious beliefs' that had no relevance to me.

At university I explored many new ideas, such as psychology, philosophy, political science, feminism, socialism, and Marxism. In these human ideologies, I sought answers for the world's problems. By my second year of university, I realised that each of these things had not delivered on the expected solutions, and I was left disappointed.

At this point God came into my life and started to make himself known to me. The Lord brought me into contact with Christians who challenged my unbelief and misconceptions about Christianity and the Bible. As I debated and argued with them, unknown to me, God was at work changing my mind. I would never have been convinced by mere human arguments, but God himself spoke to me through their words and, through his Word, the Bible.

Even so, I did not want to submit my life to God, and I didn't want him to control me. I had every intention of walking away, and living life without him, by just ignoring my growing suspicion inside me that God is real. One day God spoke to me and said: "You are either against me or for me, but I will not let you continue to live undecided, sitting on the fence. It is your choice, but you must choose today whom you will serve."

At this, I immediately repented, and submitted my life to him, saying: "What choice do you leave me? I've just heard you speak to me. What kind of a fool would I be if walk away from you now that I know you are real?"

I knew that I had received the Holy Spirit because my mind, and my life, changed immediately. I was filled with hunger for the Word of God and began to read the Bible with a completely new understanding, as though I was hearing God's thoughts. As I came to know Jesus, I loved him, yet I still hadn't fully grasped that my salvation was not based on my performance, but on what Jesus had done for me. It took some time for that old way of thinking to be corrected by what God's Word was revealing to me.

I also faced a lot of opposition within my family, particularly from my mother who was a strongly religious Orthodox woman. In the years I had been an atheist she did not fight with me but, as soon as I declared that I was now a reborn Christian and I started attending a Bible-teaching church, this became a very serious problem between us. She almost disowned me. I prayed to God and asked him to intervene because we could not have a reasonable discussion about it, and the situation was extremely distressing for both of us.

God was gracious to me and my family. First my grandmother came to know the Lord as her Saviour, and was filled by his grace, mercy, hope and love. Sometime later my mother also received the Holy Spirit and was transformed from a religious person to one who knew and loved Jesus as her personal Saviour. Many years later, at the end of his life, my father also received God's mercy. He finally gave up saying that God would accept him based on his religion and his good works and said to me: "I'm not good enough". I reminded him that none of us are good enough, and that is why we all need a Saviour. I invited him to pray with me, and to confess his need to God, and to thank him for sending Jesus to save us. I am eternally grateful to God for coming into our lives and doing for us what we could not do for ourselves. I look forward to worshipping him for all eternity, together with all my family members who have received Jesus as their Saviour.

CHAPTER SEVENTEEN

Next Steps

Read the Bible for Yourself

God gave us his word for all to understand. While some passages might be more complex than others, the basic message that God wants us to know is straightforward. So, the first thing to do is to start reading for yourself.

The quickest way is to access the Bible on the web. A great site is **biblegateway.com** which can display passages from a variety of translations, and modern languages, that are faithful to the original text. Some of the more easily readable versions are the Christian Standard Bible (CSB), the English Standard Version (ESV), and the New International Version (NIV). Pick the one you prefer for, ultimately, it's more important that you read God's word than the translation you choose.

A useful place to start is with one of the Gospels. Matthew, Mark, Luke and John are biographies of Jesus life. Mark is the shortest, and easiest to read.

As you read, I recommend you ask yourself the question: "Who do I think Jesus is?" CS Lewis (who wrote the Narnia books) suggested that there were only four possible answers to that question. He stated that Jesus is Lord, Liar, Lunatic, or Legend.

Is Jesus a Legend?

The best way to answer that question is to read the Gospel accounts. Even though miracles and amazing claims are made – such as Jesus claiming to be God, and that he would rise from the dead – they do not read like fantastic fiction or allegory. They are, instead, a realistic account of events that occurred in a specific time and place. Importantly, these books were circulated in the living memory of those who were there – who could have discredited and ended Christianity in the first Century, yet clearly did not.

Is Jesus a Lunatic?

Considering Jesus' miracles and claims, many of his contemporaries concluded that he was out of his mind, including his family (Mark 3:21). Again, by reading the accounts of his life, you will discover that not a saner person has ever lived.

Is Jesus a Liar?

In other words, was Jesus a conman? However, everything he said was true – even when he claimed he would rise from the dead. He did not take anyone's money or exploit them in any way. Further if he was a conman, he was not good at it because he was ultimately executed. Read the accounts and decide for yourself whether Jesus was speaking the truth.

Is Jesus Lord?

Jesus cannot simply be a good man, or a revolutionary, or a philanthropist. He claimed to be both God and man, the creator who came from Heaven, and returned there to rule the universe by his Father's side. If what he is saying is false, then he is either lunatic or a liar. But, once you discard the other three possibilities, only one remains – Jesus is who he says he is – the Lord of all, the giver of life, our creator and provider, whose life, death and resurrection is the only way to rescue us from sin and death.

Acknowledging that Jesus is Lord gives us confidence in him. It also invites us to serve him as he deserves, to live the abundant life for which we have been designed.

Read the Bible with someone else

It would also be a great idea to read the Bible with someone who can guide you through it. Perhaps you know someone, whose confidence is in the Bible as the Word of God. If not, then the best place to find one is at a Bible teaching Church.

Connect with a Bible teaching Church

A Church where you can regularly hear the Bible being taught will help you grow in your understanding. There is also great value in being a part of a small group Bible study, where you can ask questions and get to hear from how other people live in service of Jesus.

You can find some Bible teaching Churches listed at **www.thegospelcoalition.org/churches**

Too much information?

If all this information has been a bit overwhelming, you might find it helpful to look at a summary of God's message to us in the Bible. You will find it at **twowaystolive.com**

CHAPTER EIGHTEEN

Advice to Christian Friends

Some guidance

This chapter is for those people who have read this book to aid your Eastern Orthodox friends and relatives in their relationship with God. I'm expecting that, like me, you are convicted that salvation comes by grace through faith in Jesus Christ alone, so that your desire is for all people, everywhere, to know him. Thank you for your love for our Lord, and your Orthodox friends.

I hope this book has deepened your understanding about Orthodoxy and provided some helpful discussion starters.

In this chapter I want to offer some guidance to assist your conversations.

Prayer first

We must always remember that we cannot convince people of the truth by friendship, or clever arguments, or by understanding God's word alone. Only by God opening people's hearts and minds will anyone be saved. So, the first thing for us to do is to bring the salvation of those around us to

God in prayer. And how exciting is it to know that God is not pestered by this prayer, or reluctant to forgive! God welcomes this prayer, for his deep desire is for all to turn to him for salvation (2 Peter 3:9).

Start the Conversation

Whilst it is right to gain an understanding about Eastern Orthodoxy to inform your conversation, we must never assume that our friend holds all those positions. In fact, I think the best place to start a Gospel conversation with *any* individual is to first ask them what they currently believe.

Ask them about their traditions around Easter, Christmas, Baptisms, Weddings. Even if they don't celebrate these, or have negative things to say, ask them why, and it will help you in understanding their position. In general, Orthodox people love talking about their culture!

Try and gain an appreciation of how they come to grasp the things of God. Listen carefully – understanding your friend may involve you in a steep learning curve. Their way of knowing God may be very different to yours. Is it self-denial, participation in the Church, or living a moral life that draws them closer to God, or something else? Who are those who are particularly close to God – the monks, the priests, those who attend all the services and festivals? Can God be known at all?

Many (not just Orthodox) people may never have attempted to synthesise their thoughts about God. You may need to help them understand their position. I have found two questions helpful for this purpose.

The first I introduced in Chapter Two: "If you were to die tonight and come before God, would he let you into Heaven?" It's the question of certainty which has been central to this book. However, it helps someone consider upon what their hopes for salvation are based, and if certainty is even possible.

The second question is: "How far along are you in your spiritual journey towards peace with God?" This asks someone to consider what they really think, if it makes them closer or further away from God. It's also another way to speak of certainty, as it asks whether they think peace with God is possible.

Each of these questions helps your friend consider where they stand with God, and why – and helps you understand their thinking as well.

If you wish to know more, search the web for a training course I have written called *Evangelising Eastern Orthodoxy*. Over a number of sessions you can learn more about Eastern Orthodox doctrine, with exercises that guide you to help challenge your friends to better know Jesus and the salvation he brings.

Read the Bible with them

Most importantly, however, I would like you to read the Bible with them. My aim in writing this book has not been to replace one human authority for another, by asking them to trust my view, or yours, on how a relationship with God is possible. I want all other authorities to be overruled by the God who speaks clearly to us in his Word.

I hope this book has gone some way to challenge its readers with God's Word. But nothing is more convicting than for an individual to struggle with understanding the Scriptures themselves for, through them, God speaks to and calls people to himself.

This is where you can love your friends in the best way – by opening the Bible with them, guiding them in understanding, and answering their questions.

You could start anywhere, for the Bible is all God's word to us, testifying to salvation in Jesus Christ alone. However, I would start with a Gospel.

Mark is my first choice because it is short, and perhaps the easiest to comprehend. The aim is to answer the question repeatedly asked of us by the text – who do we think Jesus is? Is he really the God/man he claims to be? Can he be trusted when he says he died to ransom many? Can I be sure that the death of Jesus was sufficient to pay for my sins? By following him can I be confident I am acceptable to God?

If you find the prospect of opening and reading the Bible with someone a bit challenging, you could also consider using a prepared Bible Study. There are many for the Gospels – but make sure they direct you back to the text for the answers.

There are two I have found very useful. One is *Just for Starters*. It's a series of seven studies covering the basics of the Christian faith. They examine small passages, and ask simple questions, driving the points home very effectively. They do not require a high level of comprehension, and they teach someone how to read and understand the Bible in the same way as any other piece of writing.

Another is called *Tough Questions*, a series of five studies, each based on passages in Mark. As the name suggests, these are more confrontational studies that challenge the reader's ways of thinking about God. So, they are for those who can handle being pushed a bit harder in their understanding. You can find both *Just for Starters* and *Tough Questions* at **matthiasmedia. com.au**

Questions will be asked

As you talk and read with them, you should anticipate that they will raise all kinds of questions. There will be many you have heard before from others, but possibly some that have never crossed your mind. Someone's questions will always be influenced by a person's worldview, and theirs may be quite different from yours. Eastern Orthodoxy approaches God-questions in a way that is unfamiliar to you. Great importance is placed on family, tradition and culture, and these also might not be part of your personal experience.

So, when those unexpected questions arise, see them as an excellent opportunity to better understand your friend. Explain that you had never thought to ask that question, and ask them to explain why that issue is important to them.

The best answer to all questions is for you both to look again at God's word and be centred on Jesus. For instance, there are many possible ways to answer the question 'Does God exist?', but I think the best answer is to ask someone to consider Jesus' claims to be one with the Father – for that directs the questioner back to the heart of the Gospel.

If you don't have an answer to their question – just say so! Tell them you will make a note and get back to them, which is a great way to continue the conversation. Make sure you do follow up with them, after working on the answer and/or consulting a trusted friend.

Look out for my companion volume to this book called *Certainty for Life: Questions, Answers and Discussion Guide*. As the name suggests, in that you will find some suggested answers to common questions asked by those from Eastern Orthodox backgrounds.

Read this Book with them

In addition, you could also read this book with them. I have formulated dis-cussion questions for most of the chapters and included them in *Certainty for Life: Questions, Answers and Discussion Guide*. You could read a few chapters at a time, either together or individually, and use the questions to spark your discussion.

Introduce them to your Christian Friends and Teachers

It will also be of great value to them to meet other Bible believing Christians and come under sound Biblical teaching. It will help them to meet others who seek to live under the authority of God's word. They will hear different perspectives, more answers to their questions, and be encouraged to continue investigating the things of God.

A question to ask them

Should your conversations continue, you may arrive at the point where your friend understands the Biblical Gospel but expresses hesitation in making a decision to follow Christ.

I have found it helpful to lay out the elements of the Gospel, with a presentation like *Two Ways to Live* (**twowaystolive.com**), concluding with this question: "What is stopping you today from making the decision to live your life for Jesus?" As before, the aim of this question is to help them, and you, to understand the reasons for their reluctance.

It may be that there are elements of the Gospel they still cannot accept – for instance, that all people are sinful and deserve death. Identifying these elements will guide you to what to reconsider with them.

Alternatively, they may acknowledge the Gospel is true, and that repentance is imperative for salvation, but identify other stumbling blocks. Family is number one – "What will my parents/wife/cousins say?"

Linked to this is the fear of cultural betrayal. You need to understand that Orthodoxy is not primarily a belief system alone but is intimately linked to cultural identity. To be Greek is to be Orthodox, and to be Orthodox is to be Greek – and the same is true for other cultures embedded with

Orthodoxy. Deciding to follow Christ may be seen as a departure from Orthodoxy, whereas it should be understood as deciding to stand with God's people in fulfilment of our baptismal promises (see Chapter 12).

There will definitely be other objections raised. These should not be dismissed, but be handled with understanding and sensitivity. However, ultimately the answer is this – there is a cost that all pay to follow Christ, but the benefit will always outweigh it. God is calling you, through Christ, to serve him and avoid the coming judgement. Now is the opportunity to accept that the only and certain salvation is through the death and resurrection of Christ – tomorrow may be too late.

My prayers will be with you that God, by his grace, will be pleased to use your Gospel efforts to accomplish his work of reconciling many Eastern Orthodox people to their creator and redeemer.